# THE
# JEWISH
# HERITAGE
# QUIZ
# BOOK

# THE
# JEWISH HERITAGE QUIZ BOOK

ALFRED J. KOLATCH

TESTAMENT
BOOKS

New York

This 1999 edition is published by Testament Books™,
an imprint of Random House Value Publishing, Inc.,
201 East 50th Street, New York, New York 10022,
by arrangement with Jonathan David Publishers, Inc.

Testament Books™ and colophon are trademarks of
Random House Value Publishing, Inc.

Random House
New York • Toronto • London • Sydney • Auckland
http://www.randomhouse.com/

Printed and bound in the United States of America

A CIP catalog record for this book is available
from the Library of Congress.

ISBN 0-517-20581-5

8 7 6 5 4 3 2 1

# Table of Contents

## Questions

## Answers

# Introduction

Many people think of Judaism solely as a religion, while others think of it as a cultural or ethnic entity. In fact it is much more than these characterizations. As is evident from the range of subject matter covered in the nine chapters of this volume, the Jewish heritage includes the Bible and its teachings; history; the arts, sports, and entertainment; holidays, customs, and rituals; service organizations and institutions of learning; language and literature—in short, an entire way of life. The Jewish heritage is the sum total of significant contributions made, over the ages, by Jewish men and women of great talent in every field of human endeavor—from *belles lettres* and scientific discovery to politics, religion, biblical study, and philosophic inquiry.

*The Jewish Heritage Quiz Book* has been designed so that adults with varying degrees of Jewish education can test and possibly enhance their knowledge of the Jewish legacy in an informal and entertaining way. Through its hundreds of multiple-choice questions, which in themselves provide informational clues to the correct answers, one can add considerably to his or her font of knowledge. The answers themselves, which can be found in the back of the book, are also a source of interesting supplementary information.

*The Jewish Heritage Quiz Book* should be approached in a spirit of fun. The questions do not appear in any particular order—chronologically or otherwise—thus adding to the informality of the presentation. It should provide many hours of pleasure whether used either by an individual or in a group setting, where players challenge each other for a better score.

So, I invite you to refresh your memories of things once learned and perhaps forgotten and to enjoy the stimulation of new knowledge that may come your way as a result of the use of this volume.

Alfred J. Kolatch
January 2, 1995

# The Bible    1

**1.** How many books are there in the Bible?

   a. thirty-nine
   b. five
   c. sixty-three
   d. twelve

**2.** The Bible mentions several incidents in which animals spoke like people. Which of these animals spoke out?

   a. a snake
   b. a donkey
   c. a horse
   d. a cow

**3.** A number of events in the Bible lasted forty days, forty nights, or forty years. Which of the following are *not* correct?

   a. Moses was on Mount Sinai for forty days and forty nights to receive the Ten Commandments.
   b. Rain fell for forty days and forty nights when Noah was in the ark.
   c. Moses appeared before Pharaoh for forty days and forty nights.
   d. Joshua and the Israelites circled Jericho for forty days and forty nights.

**4.** Jews often speak of the Oral Law and the Written Law. To what does the Written Law refer?

   a. the Torah
   b. the Talmud
   c. the Kabbalah
   d. the Prophets

**5.** One part of the Bible is called Neviim ("Prophets").
Which of these books are included in this section?

    a.  Kings, Amos, and Hosea
    b.  Joshua, Judges, and Daniel
    c.  Samuel, Kings, and Ezra
    d.  Joshua, Judges, and Samuel

**6.** The third section of the Bible, which includes such
books as Proverbs, Psalms, Job, and the Song of Songs,
is called Ketuvim ("Holy Writings"). The Greek word
for it is

    a.  Deuteronomy
    b.  Chronicles
    c.  Hagiographa
    d.  Apocrypha

**7.** The book of the Bible that tells the story of Creation is

    a.  Genesis
    b.  Exodus
    c.  Leviticus
    d.  Numbers
    e.  Deuteronomy

**8.** The Decalogue ("Ten Words") is more popularly
known as the

    a.  Ten Plagues
    b.  Ten Commandments
    c.  Report of the Ten Tribes
    d.  Ten Rules of Conduct

9. The book of the Bible that tells the story of the Patriarchs is

    a. Genesis
    b. Exodus
    c. Leviticus
    d. Numbers
    e. Deuteronomy

10. Of these four Bible scholars, the first to write a commentary on the Five Books of Moses was

    a. Ramban
    b. Rashi
    c. Moses Mendelssohn
    d. Samson Raphael Hirsch

11. Which one of these books is *not* part of the Torah?

    a. Genesis
    b. Exodus
    c. Numbers
    d. Jeremiah

12. Which one of these books is *not* part of the Prophets?

    a. Isaiah
    b. Leviticus
    c. Amos
    d. Hosea

**13.** Fourteen books similar in style to the books of the Bible were written during the centuries immediately preceding the destruction of the Second Temple in 70 C.E. These books were not included among the official books of the Bible because they were written after the Bible was finalized (canonized). They are referred to as the

    a. Apocrypha
    b. Ketuvim
    c. Tray Asar
    d. Pseudepigrapha

**14.** The Latin translation of the Bible was written in Palestine between the years 390 and 405 C.E. by Church Father Jerome. This translation, which became the official version of the Catholic Church, is known as the

    a. Vulgate
    b. Apocrypha
    c. Zohar
    d. Incunabula

**15.** Some of these books are not part of the Bible but are part of the Apocrypha. Those that are part of the Apocrypha are

    a. Tobit
    b. Samuel
    c. Judith
    d. Susanna
    e. Joshua
    f. Esther

**16.** A synonym for Bible is

    a. Torah
    b. Prophets
    c. Holy Scriptures
    d. Apocrypha

**17.** The book of the Torah that summarizes much of what is described in other books of the Torah is

    a. Genesis
    b. Exodus
    c. Leviticus
    d. Numbers
    e. Deuteronomy

**18.** The book of the Bible that tells the story of the enslavement of the Children of Israel in Egypt is

    a. Genesis
    b. Exodus
    c. Leviticus
    d. Numbers
    e. Deuteronomy

**19.** The Latin phrase *creatio ex nihilo* refers to which of the following portions of the Bible?

    a. the first chapter of Exodus
    b. the first chapter of Genesis
    c. the first chapter of Chronicles
    d. the first chapter of Job

**20.** In addition to Song of Songs, Lamentations, Ecclesiastes, and Esther, one of the following is the fifth book in the group called the Five Scrolls. Which is it?

    a. Ruth
    b. Judith
    c. Tobit
    d. Susanna

**21.** In the Bible, God is often referred to as Yahweh or Jehovah. Some of the other biblical names by which God is known are

    a. Adama
    b. Elohim
    c. Adoshem
    d. Adonai

**22.** The most important of all God's creations was man and woman. These He created on the

    a. sixth day
    b. first day
    c. seventh day
    d. second day

**23.** The first word in the Hebrew Bible is *bereshit*. *Bereshit* means

    a. and God said
    b. in the beginning
    c. God created
    d. introducing

24. In the early pages of the Bible, we are told that God planted a garden and put Adam and Eve in that garden. The name of the garden is

    a. Garden of Sodom
    b. Garden of Eve
    c. Garden of Eden
    d. Garden of Knowledge

25. Which of these statements is false?

    a. Adam and Eve ate an apple in the Garden of Eden.
    b. Jonah was swallowed up by a whale.
    c. Mordecai was Esther's uncle.
    d. Amram was the father of Moses.

26. The names of all biblical characters have meanings. Eve means "life" and David means "friend." Whose name means "earth"?

    a. Adam
    b. Noah
    c. Jacob
    d. Reuben

27. There are two stories in the Book of Genesis about the creation of Eve, the first woman. In one, she and Adam were created at the same time. In the second she was formed from

    a. one of Adam's ribs
    b. the seed of an apple
    c. the bones of an animal
    d. the soil

**28.** The garden in which Adam and Eve lived was called
Eden. God permitted Adam to eat the fruit of any tree
except the

    a. Tree of Life
    b. Tree of Eternity
    c. Tree of Knowledge
    d. Tree of Hope

**29.** In the Bible the serpent had legs like other animals.
The serpent did something wrong and as a result was
punished. What did he do?

    a. He told Adam that he would never have
       children.
    b. He tempted Eve to eat of the fruit of the Tree
       of Knowledge.
    c. He told Adam's son to cut down all the trees.
    d. He told Adam to sacrifice his children.

**30.** Which of these famous biblical couples was deeply in
love but never married?

    a. Rebecca and Isaac
    b. Naomi and Elimelech
    c. Zipporah and Moses
    d. Delilah and Samson

**31.** Because Moses was tongue-tied, God told him to take
someone along to speak for him when he appeared before Pharaoh. Who was it?

    a. Jethro, his father-in-law
    b. Amram, his father
    c. Aaron, his brother
    d. Zipporah, his wife

**32.** Aaron, his brother Moses, and his sister Miriam were members of a tribe from which all Priests were descended. The name of that tribe is

    a. Reuben
    b. Simeon
    c. Levi
    d. Judah

**33.** When Pharaoh refused to permit the Israelites to go into the wilderness to worship God, Aaron performed a magical feat. He threw his rod on the ground and it turned into a

    a. tree
    b. snake
    c. bush
    d. frog

**34.** When Moses went up to Mount Sinai to receive the Ten Commandments, he remained there for an extended period of time. The Israelites thought that he would never come down. What did they ask Aaron to do for them?

    a. make a holy ark
    b. build a tabernacle
    c. make a god that they could worship
    d. build a golden altar

**35.** Which of these women became King David's wife after the death of her husband, Nabal, a wealthy farmer?

    a. Abigail
    b. Naomi
    c. Esther
    d. Tobit

**36.** Abraham's intended offering of Isaac as a sacrifice is known in Hebrew as the

    a. Akeda
    b. Matan Torah
    c. Mabul
    d. Aguna
    e. Mincha

**37.** Abraham never actually sacrificed his son Isaac, but in the Book of Judges one man kept his promise and did sacrifice his daughter. That man's name is

    a. Samson
    b. Jephtha
    c. Joshua
    d. Samuel

**38.** The Cave of Machpela in the town of Hebron was purchased by Abraham from Ephron the Hittite as a burial place for

    a. Isaac
    b. Ishmael
    c. Sarah
    d. Hagar

**39.** He was King Saul's uncle and the commander of his army. After Saul's death, he became attached to the court of King David. He was later killed by Joab. David composed a famous lament for him. What is his name?

    a. Abner ben Ner
    b. Joshua bin Nun
    c. Akiba ben Joseph
    d. Bezalel ben Uri

**40.** In one of the books of the Bible, there is no mention of the name of God. That book is

    a. Isaiah
    b. Jonah
    c. Genesis
    d. Esther

**41.** Abraham had two wives who are mentioned in the Bible. One was Sarah and the other was Hagar. Each had a son. Sarah's son was Isaac. What was the name of Hagar's son?

    a. Ishmael
    b. Samuel
    c. Esau
    d. Jacob

**42.** Ur of the Chaldees, an ancient Babylonian city, was the home of a well-known biblical character before his departure for Haran. That person is

    a. Joshua
    b. Abraham
    c. Moses
    d. Esau

**43.** Which of these men was Rebecca's father-in-law?

    a. Abraham
    b. Isaac
    c. Jacob
    d. Joseph

44. Ishmael, Abraham's son, was the brother of Isaac. Ishmael's mother's name was

    a. Sarah
    b. Hagar
    c. Rebecca
    d. Leah

45. Which of the women listed below were *not* married to Abraham, Isaac, or Jacob?

    a. Dinah
    b. Miriam
    c. Rebecca
    d. Leah

46. Which one of the following people is not mentioned in the Bible?

    a. Daniel
    b. Balaam
    c. Elisha
    d. Hillel

47. Which one of these people lived first?

    a. Esau
    b. Joseph
    c. Abraham
    d. Adam

48. An ancient people mentioned several times in the Bible was very hostile to the Children of Israel. This tribe was named

    a. Hur
    b. Midian
    c. Amalek
    d. Edom

**49.** By occupation, he was a herdsman and a sycamore tree pruner. What was the name of this eighth-century B.C.E. prophet who was a Judean?

    a. Jeremiah
    b. Isaiah
    c. Amos
    d. Joel

**50.** The idea that Moses had two horns growing out of his forehead was first expressed in a piece of sculpture by

    a. Leonardo da Vinci
    b. Jacob Epstein
    c. Michelangelo
    d. Jacques Lipchitz

**51.** One group of people in the Bible was punished for trying to build a tower that would reach into heaven. What was their punishment?

    a. The bricks that they used fell and killed them.
    b. They began to speak different languages and couldn't understand each other.
    c. It rained for forty days and forty nights and they couldn't work.
    d. They were destroyed by a bolt of lightning.

**52.** Hananiah, Mishael, and Azariah were friends with a person who was a close advisor to Nebuchadnezzar during the Babylonian Exile (sixth century B.C.E.). The name of this person is

    a. Nehemiah
    b. Ezra
    c. Daniel
    d. Jonah

**53.** Daniel refused to worship the idols set up by King Darius. As a result, the king

    a. banished him from the country
    b. cast him into a lion's den
    c. threw him into a fiery furnace
    d. praised him for being loyal to God

**54.** Dinah, the daughter of Jacob, was seduced by Shechem, the son of Hamor. Two of her brothers were very angry when they learned of this. Who were they?

    a. Simeon and Levi
    b. Levi and Ephraim
    c. Judah and Isaac
    d. Dan and Joseph

**55.** Of the twelve tribes among whom Palestine was divided when the Children of Israel entered Canaan after the death of Moses, two were not the names of Jacob's twelve sons. These two tribes were

    a. Reuben and Simeon
    b. Ephraim and Manasseh
    c. Gad and Asher
    d. Judah and Levi

**56.** Chapter 19 of the Book of Leviticus repeats in essence the Ten Commandments which appear in Exodus 20 and Deuteronomy 5. Chapter 19 is known as the

    a. Code of Moses
    b. Holiness Code
    c. Code of Abraham
    d. Code of Hammurabi

**57.** In Leviticus 19, laws are mentioned relating to the treatment of animals. What does the Bible say about plowing the field with a team made up of an ox and a donkey?

   a. The ox should be the same size as the donkey.
   b. The two should not be used together.
   c. The donkey should always be harnessed on the right side of the ox.
   d. The two should be used together only during a sabbatical year.

**58.** Ludwig Lazarus Zamenhof (1859-1917) translated the Bible into a language of his own invention. The name of that language is

   a. Ugaritic
   b. Swahili
   c. Esperanto
   d. Ge'ez

**59.** The Book of Leviticus (25:8) speaks of the fiftieth year as a special year in which slaves are freed and all land purchases of the previous fifty years must be returned to the original owner. The name of this year is the

   a. shemita year
   b. jubilee year
   c. leap year
   d. year of redemption

**60.** Isaac and his wife, Rebecca, had twin sons. What were their names?

   a. Shem and Japhet
   b. Cain and Abel
   c. Jacob and Esau
   d. Joseph and Benjamin

**61.** Esau was angry with his brother, Jacob, because he claimed that Jacob had stolen from him his

    a. bows and arrows
    b. birthright
    c. hunting equipment
    d. coat of many colors

**62.** When Jacob was finally free to leave his father-in-law's home, Laban accused him of stealing his

    a. wife
    b. daughters
    c. idols
    d. animals

**63.** The Hebrew title of a book often differs from its English title because in ancient times Jews sometimes chose the first or second significant word of a book's opening sentence as its title. Which of these biblical books' titles correlate most closely in meaning?

    a. Bereshit and Genesis
    b. Shemot and Exodus
    c. Va-yikra and Leviticus
    d. Be-midbar and Numbers
    e. Devarim and Deuteronomy

**64.** A Greek translation of the Bible was composed in Alexandria, Egypt, in the middle of the third century B.C.E. It was executed at the command of Ptolemy, ruler of Egypt, who had ordered Jewish scholars to do the translating. The number of scholars employed was

    a. ten
    b. twenty
    c. fifty
    d. seventy

**65.** One man in the Bible was so in love with a woman that he was willing to work for her father for fourteen years in order to win her hand in marriage. Who was the man and for whom did he work?

    a. David worked for Saul in order to marry Michal.
    b. Jacob worked for Laban in order to marry Rachel.
    c. Adam worked for Cain in order to marry Eve.
    d. Aaron worked for Moses in order to marry Deborah.

**66.** Jacob had four wives. Two of them were Rachel and Leah. Who were the other two?

    a. Sarah and Rebecca
    b. Bilhah and Zilpah
    c. Dina and Eve
    d. Miriam and Zipporah

**67.** Wars were very common in biblical days. Some interesting laws on how to act in wartime are laid down in the Book of Deuteronomy. The Bible states that in wartime

    a. fruit trees may not be cut down
    b. prisoners may not be taken
    c. soldiers who are afraid should be sent home
    d. newly married men should be exempted from service

**68.** Jacob had twelve sons. Benjamin, born near Bethlehem, was the youngest. Benjamin's mother had one other son. Who was the mother and who was her other son?

  a. Rachel was the mother and her other son was Joseph.
  b. Leah was the mother and her other son was Reuben.
  c. Zilpah was the mother and her other son was Joseph.
  d. Miriam was the mother and her other son was Aaron.

**69.** Many characters in the Bible gave gifts to others. A coat was given to whom by whom?

  a. Abel gave a coat to God.
  b. Jacob gave a coat to Joseph.
  c. Joseph gave a coat to Jacob.
  d. Esau gave a coat to Isaac.

**70.** An Israelite Judge vowed that if he returned safely from battling the Ammonites, he would sacrifice the first thing that came out of his house. Upon his return, he was met by his daughter. The name of the Judge was

  a. Jephthah
  b. Joshua
  c. Samson
  d. Ehud

71. Samson is generally assumed to be the strong man of the Bible. Who else in the Bible was so strong that he was singlehandedly able to roll a huge stone from the mouth of a well?

    a. Joshua
    b. Jacob
    c. Joseph
    d. Judah

72. This man was the king of Israel from about 876 to 853 B.C.E. His wife's name was Jezebel. Who was he?

    a. Saul
    b. Ahab
    c. David
    d. Jeroboam

73. When Joseph allowed his brothers to return to their father, Jacob, he had a servant plant a silver goblet in the knapsack of one of the brothers. The name of that brother is

    a. Benjamin
    b. Judah
    c. Reuben
    d. Dan

74. Joseph was able to interpret Pharaoh's dreams because he noticed that certain numbers kept recurring. The number that came up most frequently in the king's dreams was

    a. five
    b. six
    c. seven
    d. ten

**75.** The shortest book in the Bible has only

    a. four chapters
    b. three chapters
    c. two chapters
    d. one chapter

**76.** The Persian queen, Vashti, wife of King Ahasueros, refused to appear before the king at a banquet as commanded. As punishment, the king

    a. beheaded her
    b. banned her from his presence
    c. forgave her
    d. sent her back to her father

**77.** When Joseph was brought to Egypt by the Ishmaelites, he was sold as a slave to an important person in the king's court. Who was the man and what position did he hold?

    a. Ephraim, the Egyptian treasurer
    b. Ephraim, the king's courier
    c. Potifar, captain of the king's guard
    d. Ishmael, the king's baker

**78.** While imprisoned in Egypt, Joseph interpreted the dreams of the Pharaoh's butler and baker. Soon afterward, the baker was hung and the butler was restored to his position. How did this affect Joseph's future?

    a. Joseph became the baker and was released from prison.
    b. The butler told the king that Joseph was able to interpret dreams. Joseph interpreted the king's dreams and was rewarded.
    c. Pharaoh freed Joseph from prison and sent him back to his father in the Land of Canaan.
    d. Joseph was released from prison and appointed treasurer of Egypt.

**79.** Pharaoh had a dream that no one could interpret. Joseph was finally called in, and he succeeded in interpreting it. The dream concerned

    a. seven lean cows and seven fat ones
    b. three lean ears of grain and three fat ones
    c. seven lean horses and seven fat ones
    d. seven fat horses and three lean cows

**80.** The ark that was carried through the desert for forty years after the exodus from Egypt

    a. was an empty box
    b. contained a Torah
    c. contained the Ten Commandments
    d. contained the High Priest's crown

**81.** The triennial cycle refers to a system of reading the Torah. According to this system it takes three years to

    a. read the entire Torah
    b. read all the Prophets
    c. give all men aliyot
    d. read all of the books in the Hagiographa

**82.** The total number of positive and negative commandments (*mitzvot*) in the Torah is 613. The Hebrew term that describes these commandments is

    a. B'nai Mitzva
    b. Bar Mitzva
    c. Aseret Ha-dibrot
    d. Taryag Mitzvot

**83.** Jacob wrestled with a man all night long and defeated him. As a result Jacob was given a new name. That name is

    a. Aaron
    b. Noah
    c. Yisrael
    d. Yaakov

**84.** During years of famine in the Middle East, Jacob and his family lived in Canaan. Joseph was a high official in Egypt at the time. Jacob sent his sons to Egypt to buy food. What happened when the brothers faced Joseph for the first time?

    a. Joseph recognized his brothers immediately.
    b. The brothers recognized Joseph immediately.
    c. Only Joseph and Benjamin recognized each other.
    d. Only Joseph and Asher recognized each other.

**85.** After Joseph revealed his identity to his brothers, he sent them back home to Canaan to bring their father Jacob and their families down to Egypt. Joseph set aside one city in Egypt in which his family would live. That city was

    a. Canaan
    b. Goshen
    c. Shechem
    d. Cairo

**86.** Joseph was a dreamer. His brothers hated him because in his dreams he was more important than they. Which of the following did Joseph dream?

    a.  that the sun, moon, and stars bowed down to him

    b.  that a ladder with him on top reached to heaven

    c.  that a rainbow appeared in the sky at his command

    d.  that seven thin cows swallowed seven fat ones

**87.** Absalom, the third son of King David, was tall and handsome, with a long mane of hair. One day while riding his mule,

    a.  the mule tripped and Absalom was killed

    b.  Absalom fell off the mule, which had broken its leg

    c.  Absalom's hair got caught in the branches of a tree

    d.  Absalom was struck by a bolt of lightning

**88.** One biblical character had friends named Eliphaz the Temanite, Bildad the Shuhite, and Zophar the Naamathite. That character's name is

    a.  Joshua

    b.  Jeremiah

    c.  Job

    d.  Daniel

**89.** One prophet disobeyed God by going to Tarshish instead of to Nineveh as ordered. In the course of time, he was

    a.  thrown into a fiery furnace

    b.  thrown into a deep pit

    c.  thrown into a lion's den

    d.  swallowed up by a big fish

**90.** The man who led the Israelites when the walls of Jericho came tumbling down was

    a.  Aaron
    b.  Moses
    c.  Joshua
    d.  David

**91.** The book of the Bible in which the duties of the Priests (Kohanim) are detailed is

    a.  Genesis
    b.  Exodus
    c.  Leviticus
    d.  Numbers
    e.  Deuteronomy

**92.** Abraham had a nephew whose name was Lot. Lot's wife is famous because she looked backwards and, as a result, turned into a pillar of salt. What did Lot's wife see when she looked backwards?

    a.  She saw Jacob's ladder reaching to the heavens.
    b.  She saw Cain kill Abel but did not reveal what she saw.
    c.  She saw the wicked cities of Sodom and Gomorrah being destroyed.
    d.  She saw Moses standing on Mount Sinai.

**93.** While in the desert, the Children of Israel complained that they were hungry. God sent food in the form of dew which lay on the ground each morning. It tasted like wafers made with honey. What did the Israelites call it?

    a.  lechem
    b.  geffen
    c.  manna
    d.  matza

94. The number of Jacob's descendants who came to Egypt and the number of elders Moses appointed to assist him were the same. That number is

    a. forty
    b. fifty
    c. sixty
    d. seventy

95. There are four Matriarchs in Judaism. Sarah, Rachel, and Rebecca are three. The fourth was married to Jacob. Her name is

    a. Miriam
    b. Dinah
    c. Leah
    d. Zipporah

96. A famous incident in the Book of Numbers concerns the daughters of Zelophehad. Their father died and left no sons. They wanted to inherit their father's property, but couldn't under the law. As a result, the law was changed so that

    a. daughters could inherit if they promised to marry within one year
    b. if a man dies without leaving a son, a daughter inherits his property
    c. if a man dies without leaving a son, his wife inherits his property

97. Which of the following groups of three women were related to Moses?

    a. Zipporah, Jochebed, Miriam
    b. Miriam, Jochebed, Dinah
    c. Jochebed, Rachel, Miriam
    d. Ruth, Naomi, Delilah

**98.** When Aaron threw his staff to the ground, it turned into a snake. Among those watching was one very important person. Who was it?

    a. Jethro, the father-in-law of Moses
    b. Jochebed, the sister of Moses
    c. Pharaoh, the king of Egypt
    d. Amram, the father of Moses

**99.** Pharaoh commanded that all newborn boys of the Israelites be killed. The mother of Moses wanted to save her son, so she decided to hide him

    a. in the Temple in Jerusalem
    b. behind a tree in the Garden of Eden
    c. in a basket among the bulrushes of the Nile
    d. in Pharaoh's palace

**100.** Three men played an important part in the life of Moses. They were all related to him. Who were they?

    a. Jethro, Amram, and Joseph
    b. Aaron, Amram, and Ephraim
    c. Aaron, Jethro, and Amram
    d. Joshua, Bezalel, and Aaron

**101.** When the Israelites were in the desert, they had no water. God commanded Moses and Aaron to speak to the rock so that water would come forth. Moses disobeyed God. What did he do?

    a. He built a Golden Calf on top of the rock.
    b. He struck the rock with his staff.
    c. He covered the rock with sand.
    d. He hit the rock with his sandals.

**102.** The book of the Bible called the Song of Songs is also referred to as

    a. Ecclesiastes
    b. Canticles
    c. Chronicles
    d. Proverbs

**103.** The burning bush, described in the Book of Exodus, was unusual because it

    a. provided Moses with light to read by for forty nights
    b. burned but was not consumed
    c. was the spot on which the Ten Commandments were enunciated
    d. produced manna

**104.** Zipporah was the wife of Moses. She was also the daughter of Jethro, a Priest of Midian. Moses and Zipporah had two sons. Who were they?

    a. Gershom and Eliezer
    b. Bezalel and Hur
    c. Nadav and Avihu
    d. Reuben and Simeon

**105.** Most of the members of the Tribe of Levi were employed in occupations connected with the Tabernacle. They derived their livelihood from

    a. the half-shekel that was collected
    b. the proceeds of the sale of the urim and tumim
    c. the tithes that were collected
    d. contributions made by people who received aliyot

**106.** Many people in the Bible lived for a very long time. One man reached 969 years. He was Noah's grandfather. What was his name?

    a. Shem
    b. Lot
    c. Methuselah
    d. Japheth

**107.** On one particular holiday the biblical story of Esther is read. The story is hand-lettered on a parchment scroll called the Megilla. It is read in the synagogue on

    a. Purim eve only
    b. Purim morning only
    c. Purim evening and morning
    d. Passover after the Seder

**108.** Twelve books of the Bible are known collectively as the Minor Prophets. One of those twelve books is named after the prophet

    a. Amos
    b. Ezekiel
    c. Isaiah
    d. Jeremiah

**109.** Which of the following biblical characters had their name changed?

    a. Abraham
    b. Sarah
    c. Moses
    d. Daniel

110. Over the years, Jews have had many enemies who vowed their annihilation. The one whose name is jeered when it is mentioned during a synagogue service is

    a. Haman
    b. Amalek
    c. Pharaoh
    d. Torquemada

111. This person was the wife of Elimelech. Her two children were named Machlon and Chilion. Her daughter-in-law's name was Ruth. What is the woman's name?

    a. Esther
    b. Dinah
    c. Naomi
    d. Miriam

112. A prophet once reprimanded King David for having sent his captain, Uriah the Hittite, to the front lines. Uriah was killed and David married his wife, Bathsheba. The name of the prophet is

    a. Isaiah
    b. Hillel
    c. Nathan
    d. Samuel

113. In the Bible, we read of persons who vowed not to drink intoxicating liquor or to have their hair cut. Sometimes parents made the vow for their children. The persons subject to such vows were called

    a. Amalekites
    b. Nazirites
    c. Karaites
    d. Sadducees

**114.** Tefilin, or phylacteries, which are worn by boys over the age of thirteen, contain four handwritten portions from the Bible. These passages are found in the books of

    a. Exodus and Deuteronomy
    b. Genesis and Joshua
    c. Isaiah and Jeremiah
    d. Leviticus and Judges

**115.** The three sons of Noah who were in the ark with him were

    a. Shem, Ham, and Japheth
    b. Reuben, Simeon, and Levi
    c. Moses, Aaron, and Joshua
    d. Shadrach, Meshach, and Abed-nego

**116.** God promised Noah that He would not bring another flood upon the earth. The Bible says that as a reminder of that promise something unusual periodically appears in the sky. What is it?

    a. the sun, the moon, and the stars all at the same time
    b. a rainbow of many colors
    c. the face of the man in the moon
    d. the sun being eclipsed by the moon

**117.** Of Noah's sons, Ham was the least kind and caring. This was manifest when he

    a. got drunk
    b. stole from his brothers
    c. mistreated his mother
    d. didn't cover his father's body when it was naked

**118.** Before the flood came, Noah built an ark. He lived in it for 150 days, until the flood was over. Before Noah emerged from the ark, he sent two birds at different times to see if it was safe to leave. Which birds did he send?

    a. a raven and a robin
    b. a swallow and a raven
    c. a raven and a dove
    d. a woodpecker and a dove

**119.** Which book of the Bible gives the primary account of the wanderings of the Israelites in the desert?

    a. Genesis
    b. Exodus
    c. Leviticus
    d. Numbers
    e. Deuteronomy

**120.** This fearless ninth-century B.C.E. prophet did not hesitate to denounce King Ahab and his wife, Jezebel, for their idolatrous ways. He is mentioned prominently in the Passover Seder service. His name is

    a. Elijah
    b. Elisha
    c. Jeremiah
    d. Nathan

**121.** Pithom and Raamses were the names of

    a. major ministers of Pharaoh
    b. friends of Mordecai and Esther
    c. cities built by the Israelites when they were slaves in Egypt
    d. cities in which Joseph settled his family

**122.** Which one of these people is *not* mentioned in the Bible?

    a. Ruth
    b. Joshua
    c. Daniel
    d. Akiba
    e. Korah
    f. Deborah

**123.** Moses tried to persuade Pharaoh to free the Children of Israel. Pharaoh promised time and again that he would free them, but he did not keep his promises. After ten plagues, Pharaoh finally let the Israelites go. Which was the tenth plague?

    a. the plague of blood
    b. the plague of the firstborn
    c. the plague of darkness
    d. the plague of frogs

**124.** Which of the following animals or insects were *not* involved in any of the ten plagues visited upon the Egyptians while the Israelites were enslaved in Egypt?

    a. caterpillars
    b. bees
    c. frogs
    d. lice
    e. locusts

**125.** Ruth, the daughter-in-law of Naomi in the Book of Ruth, was born a

    a. Jewess
    b. Moabitess
    c. Persian
    d. Greek

**126.** Saul, the first king of Israel, was succeeded by David, who was his

    a. father
    b. son-in-law
    c. uncle
    d. cousin

**127.** Samson killed the Philistines with the jawbone of an ass. What implement did the son of Jesse use to kill his opponent?

    a. a bow and arrow
    b. a sword
    c. a slingshot
    d. a spear

**128.** Sodom and Gomorrah are mentioned in the Book of Genesis as

    a. the hometowns of Esau and Jacob
    b. the burial sites of Rachel and Leah
    c. places of extreme wickedness
    d. places of sacred altars

# Biblical Quotables 2

1. Who said this to whom? "Behold I am at the point of death. What profit shall the birthright bring me?"

   a. Lot to Abraham
   b. Esau to Jacob
   c. Jacob to Esau
   d. Reuben to Joseph

2. "Am I a dog that you come against me with sticks?" This question was posed by

   a. Moses, when he faced Pharaoh
   b. Abel, before Cain killed him
   c. Goliath, when he saw David
   d. Samson, when he was attacked by the Philistines

3. "Whoever is for the Lord, let him follow me" was the battle cry of Mattathias as he launched a rebellion against the Syrian-Greeks, who had desecrated the Temple in Jerusalem. Which earlier biblical figure used a similar battle cry?

   a. Jephthah
   b. Solomon
   c. Joshua
   d. Moses

4. "The voice is the voice of Jacob, but the hands are the hands of Esau." Who made this statement?

   a. Esau, when he approached Isaac to be blessed
   b. Isaac to Abraham, when Abraham was given some food
   c. Isaac, when Jacob approached him for a blessing
   d. Isaac to Abraham, when Isaac was to be sacrificed

**5.** "Is your father alive? Do you have another brother?" Who asked this of whom?

    a. Judah of Joseph
    b. Joseph of Jacob
    c. Joseph of his brothers
    d. Pharaoh of Joseph

**6.** "Go forth from your native land and from your father's house to the land that I will show you." To whom did God issue this command?

    a. Jacob
    b. Isaac
    c. Abram
    d. Noah

**7.** "Here comes that dreamer! Come now, let us kill him and throw him into one of those pits." Who said this to whom?

    a. Esau to his servant
    b. the servants of Pharaoh to each other
    c. the brothers of Joseph to each other
    d. Pharaoh's servants to one another

**8.** "There is no one as discerning and as wise as you. You shall be in charge of my court, and by your command shall all my people be directed." Who said this to whom?

    a. Ahasueros to Mordecai
    b. Pharaoh to Joseph
    c. Pharaoh to Jacob
    d. Pharaoh to Moses

9. "Cursed be the day I was born and the night on which it was announced: a male child is being born." Who uttered these words?

    a. Solomon
    b. David
    c. Job
    d. Moses

10. Jacob had a dream in which he saw angels ascending and descending a ladder that reached from earth to heaven. Jacob said: "Surely, the Lord is in this place, and I did not know it." He named that place

    a. Beth El
    b. Canaan
    c. Shechem
    d. Jerusalem

11. Fill in the missing word from this popular quotation from the Book of Psalms: "Those who sow in _____ shall reap with songs of joy."

    a. sorrow
    b. happiness
    c. gladness
    d. tears

12. "My son Absalom! O my son, my son Absalom! If only I had died instead of you! O Absalom, my son, my son!" Who uttered this cry of despair?

    a. Saul
    b. Samuel
    c. David
    d. Jonathan

13. "The Lord is my Shepherd, I shall not want" was spoken by

    a. Solomon
    b. Ecclesiastes
    c. Mordecai
    d. David

14. "Cast your bread upon the waters, for after many days you will find it." In which book of the Bible is this statement found?

    a. Ecclesiastes
    b. Proverbs
    c. Psalms
    d. Exodus

15. Which of the minor prophets asked these rhetorical questions: "Have we not all one Father? Did not one God create us all? Why then do we deal unkindly with one another?"

    a. Joel
    b. Malachi
    c. Amos
    d. Jeremiah

16. Father and son went to Mount Moriah. The son said: "Here is the firestone and the wood, but where is the sheep for the sacrifice?" The father answered: "God will provide it." Who was the father and who was the son?

    a. Abraham was the father and Isaac was the son
    b. Jacob was the father and Esau was the son
    c. Abraham was the father and Jacob was the son
    d. Jacob was the father and Benjamin was the son

17. "They shall beat their swords into plowshares and their spears into pruning hooks" is a hope for universal peace expressed by two prophets. They are

    a. Isaiah and Jeremiah
    b. Isaiah and Amos
    c. Ezekiel and Isaiah
    d. Micah and Isaiah

18. "Of every tree of the garden you are free to eat, but as for the tree of knowledge of good and evil, you must not eat; for as soon as you eat of it you shall die." These words were spoken by

    a. God to Adam
    b. God to Eve
    c. the snake to Eve
    d. God to Cain

19. "If I find within the city of Sodom fifty innocent people, I will forgive the whole place for their sake." Who said this to whom?

    a. God to Satan
    b. God to Abraham
    c. Abraham to God
    d. King Solomon to David

20. "Vanity of vanities, all is vanity" is a famous verse that appears at the beginning of the

    a. Book of Proverbs
    b. Book of Psalms
    c. Book of Ecclesiastes
    d. Book of Isaiah

21. "Lazy one, go to the ant, study its ways and grow wise." These are the words of

    a. Solomon
    b. David
    c. Jeremiah
    d. Isaiah

22. "The Lord gave and the Lord has taken away; blessed be the name of the Lord." These words were uttered by

    a. Abraham
    b. Jacob
    c. Job
    d. David

23. "There hath not come a razor upon my head; for I have been a Nazirite unto God from my mother's womb. If I be shaven, then my strength will go from me and I shall become weak, and be like any other man!" Who said this to whom?

    a. Samson to Delilah
    b. David to Jonathan
    c. Jonathan to Saul
    d. Moses to Joshua

24. "And seek the welfare of the city to which I have exiled you and pray to the Lord in its behalf, for in its prosperity you shall prosper." Which of the following prophets said this?

    a. Isaiah
    b. Amos
    c. Joel
    d. Jeremiah

**25.** "My God, my God [Eli, Eli], why hast thou forsaken me!" This plea can be found in one of the

    a. psalms of David
    b. perorations of Moses
    c. protestations of King Saul
    d. speeches of Job

**26.** "I have never been a man of words. . . I am slow of speech and slow of tongue." Who said this to whom?

    a. Moses to God
    b. Moses to Aaron
    c. Aaron to Moses
    d. Joshua to Moses

**27.** "Do not come closer. Remove your sandals from your feet, for the place on which you stand is holy ground." Who said this to whom?

    a. an angel to Moses
    b. God to Moses
    c. Aaron to Moses
    d. Moses to Pharaoh

**28.** In chapter 31 of the Book of Proverbs some very complimentary things are said about a woman who is a good wife and a good mother. She is referred to as a

    a. woman of valor
    b. woman of honor
    c. woman of courage
    d. woman of beauty

29. "You have come against me with a sword and a spear and a javelin, but I come against you in the name of the Lord of Hosts." Who said this to whom?

    a. David to Saul
    b. Saul to David
    c. David to Goliath
    d. Samson to a Philistine

30. "Drink, my lord...I will also draw [water] for your camels until they finish drinking" was spoken by whom to whom?

    a. Rebecca to Abraham's servant
    b. Rebecca to Isaac
    c. Sarah to Abraham
    d. Rachel to Jacob

31. Situated in Independence Hall, Philadelphia, Pennsylvania, the Liberty Bell was first rung on July 8, 1776 to announce the signing of the Declaration of Independence. Which of these words from the Bible are inscribed on the bell?

    a. "Proclaim liberty throughout the land"
    b. "Give me liberty or give me death"
    c. "My country 'tis of thee"
    d. "Let my people go"

32. "Let us not take his life...cast him into the pit out in the wilderness" was spoken by

    a. Reuben
    b. Judah
    c. Benjamin
    d. Ephraim

**33.** The statement "My brother is a hairy man and I am smooth-skinned" was made by whom to whom?

    a. Dinah to Benjamin
    b. Joseph to Leah
    c. Jacob to Rebecca
    d. Reuben to Joseph

**34.** "Joseph is still alive! I must go see him before I die!" Who said this to whom?

    a. Benjamin to Jacob
    b. Jacob to his sons
    c. Jacob to Reuben
    d. Jacob to Judah

**35.** "Let us build a city whose top may reach the heavens" is the beginning of a famous story about people who wanted to establish a name for themselves. The story is about

    a. the Tower of Babel
    b. Jacob's Ladder
    c. Pithom and Raamses
    d. the pyramids of Egypt

**36.** Cain and Abel were brothers. Cain was a farmer and Abel was a shepherd. Cain was jealous of Abel and killed him. When God asked Cain, "Where is thy brother?" his answer was

    a. "My brother went to Dothan to see his father."
    b. "Am I my brother's keeper?"
    c. "My brother went to visit Noah."
    d. "My brother is at home."

**37.** Who said this to whom? "Reuben, you are my first-born, my might and the first fruit of my vigor."

    a. Joseph to Reuben
    b. Abraham to Reuben
    c. Jacob to Reuben
    d. Isaac to Reuben

**38.** Who said this to whom? "Let me swallow, I pray thee, some of the red, red pottage, for I am famished."

    a. Esau to Jacob
    b. Jacob to Esau
    c. Isaac to Esau
    d. Esau to Isaac

**39.** One of the great scholars of the first century B.C.E. is credited with being the author of the Golden Rule in its negative form: "What is hateful to you, do not do to others." The name of the scholar is

    a. Shammai
    b. Akiba
    c. Hillel
    d. Gamaliel

**40.** "How goodly are thy tents, O Jacob, thy tabernacles, O Israel." Who made this statement?

    a. the heathen prophet Balaam
    b. the Hebrew prophet Amos
    c. the Hebrew prophet Isaiah
    d. the Hebrew prophet Elijah

41. "Four score and seven years ago. . ." is the way Lincoln's Gettysburg Address begins. One of the books in the Bible uses a similar figure of speech: "The length of our life is seventy years, or by reason of strength, four score years...." In which book of the Bible are these words found?

    a. Genesis
    b. Isaiah
    c. Psalms
    d. Proverbs

42. Which character in the Bible, famous for his or her victories over the Philistines, made the statement, "With the jawbone of an ass, heaps upon heaps; With the jawbone of an ass have I smitten a thousand men!"?

    a. David
    b. Deborah
    c. Samson
    d. Miriam

43. "By the sweat of your brow shall you eat bread" was said by whom to whom?

    a. God to Adam
    b. God to Eve
    c. the snake to Adam
    d. Cain to Abel

44. "Every boy that is born you shall cast into the Nile, but let every girl live." Who issued this command to whom?

    a. God to Moses
    b. Abraham to Isaac
    c. Pharaoh to all his people
    d. Pharaoh to Miriam

**45.** "Go into the ark with your entire household, for you alone have I found righteous before Me in this generation." Who said this to whom?

    a. God to Abraham
    b. God to Moses
    c. God to Noah
    d. Noah to Abraham

**46.** A book of the Bible begins: "There lived a man in the Land of Uz…. There were born to him seven sons and three daughters…. His property was 7,000 sheep, 3,000 camels, 500 yoke of oxen…. and a very large household of slaves." What is the man's name?

    a. Amos
    b. Job
    c. Isaiah
    d. Joshua

**47.** Who said to whom, "This is my son's coat! A wild animal devoured him! Joseph was torn by a wild beast!"?

    a. Jacob to his wife Rachel
    b. Jacob to his sons
    c. Jacob to his wife Leah
    d. Jacob to his son Reuben

**48.** "Behold, you are with child and will bear a son, and you shall call him Ishmael" was said by whom to whom?

    a. an angel to Hagar
    b. Abraham to Sarah
    c. Abraham to Hagar
    d. God to Hagar

**49.** "Take thou thy son, thy only son whom thou lovest, and go to Mount Moriah and offer him as a sacrifice." Who said this to whom?

    a. God to Abraham
    b. Abraham to Isaac
    c. God to Jacob
    d. Satan to Abraham

**50.** Chapter 19 of the Book of Leviticus is called the Holiness Code. Which of the following verses appears in this chapter of the Bible?

    a. "Holy, holy, holy is the Lord, God of hosts."
    b. "Thou shalt love thy neighbor as thyself."
    c. "The Lord is my Shepherd, I shall not want."
    d. "Honor thy father and thy mother."

**51.** "Please let your servant remain as a slave to my lord instead of the boy, and let the boy go back with his brothers." Who requested this of whom?

    a. Judah of Pharaoh
    b. Joseph of Pharaoh
    c. Reuben of Joseph
    d. Judah of Joseph

**52.** "I had another dream. This time the sun, the moon, and eleven stars are bowing down to me." Who related this to whom?

    a. Reuben to his father
    b. Joseph to Jacob
    c. Joseph to his brothers
    d. Pharaoh to Joseph

53. The last five of the Ten Commandments begin with the words "Thou shalt not." Which of the following is *not* one of these five commandments?

    a. Thou shalt not work on the Sabbath
    b. Thou shalt not steal
    c. Thou shalt not covet
    d. Thou shalt not murder

54. "Man does not live by bread alone" was said by

    a. God to Moses
    b. Moses to the Children of Israel
    c. God to the Children of Israel
    d. Moses to Joshua

55. "The wolf shall dwell with the lamb, and the leopard shall lie down with the kid" was uttered by the prophet

    a. Jeremiah
    b. Isaiah
    c. Samuel
    d. Elijah

56. "Fetch me a sword.... and cut the live child in two, and give half to one and half to the other." Who said this to whom?

    a. Solomon to two fathers
    b. Solomon to two prostitutes
    c. David to two mothers
    d. David to two prostitutes

57. Who spoke the words "There is nothing new under the sun"?

    a. Solomon
    b. Moses
    c. Joshua
    d. Elijah

**58.** "Lazybones, go to the _____, study its ways, and grow wise." The missing word is

    a. lion
    b. ant
    c. fox
    d. crow

**59.** "So teach us to number our days that we get us a heart of _____." The missing word is

    a. understanding
    b. wisdom
    c. love
    d. compassion

**60.** "Behold, how good and pleasant it is for breathren to dwell together in _____." The missing word is

    a. unity
    b. peace
    c. love
    d. harmony

# Holidays, Customs, and Rituals 3

1. The Oneg Shabbat ("Sabbath Delight"), originally a gathering held late on Saturday afternoon, was inaugurated in Palestine by a well-known poet and author to encourage Jews to participate in cultural activities. The man who conceived the idea was

    a. Saul Steinberg
    b. Chaim Nachman Bialik
    c. Chaim Weizmann
    d. Shaul Tchernichovsky

2. The ring ritual at a traditional Jewish wedding ceremony is properly carried out if the ring

    a. is placed on the forefinger of the bride's right hand
    b. is placed on the fourth finger of the bride's left hand
    c. has only one diamond in it
    d. has no gems in it

3. The holiday on which it is mandatory to eat bitter herbs is

    a. Chanuka
    b. Sukkot
    c. Passover
    d. Simchat Torah

4. The movie *Schindler's List* ends with a long procession of mourners leaving an object on Schindler's grave. The object is a

    a. flower
    b. clump of grass
    c. photograph
    d. stone

**5.** Shavuot, the third major holiday mentioned in the Book of Leviticus is known as the Feast of Weeks, because it

    a. takes place seven weeks after Passover
    b. takes place seven weeks after Purim
    c. lasts for seven weeks
    d. takes place five weeks after Passover

**6.** A Bar Mitzva ceremony can be held only at a religious service at which

    a. a cantor is present
    b. the Torah is read
    c. a rabbi is present
    d. a haftara is read

**7.** Small leather boxes containing pieces of parchment on which passages from the Bible have been handwritten are worn by adult Jews during weekday morning services. These are called

    a. tefilin
    b. talitot
    c. mezuzot
    d. tzitzit

**8.** Adloyada is the name of a celebration that takes place on

    a. Purim
    b. Passover
    c. Chanukah
    d. Sukkot

9.  According to Jewish law, when naming a newborn baby it is

    a.  not permissible to name it after a living grand-father
    b.  not permissible to name it after a living grand-mother
    c.  permissible to name it after anyone, living or dead
    d.  not permissible to name it after a living mother or father

10. Once a year a ceremony is held during which sins are symbolically cast into a body of flowing water. The ceremony is called

    a.  Havdala
    b.  Kiddush
    c.  Tashlich
    d.  Mechila

11. The Bedikat Chametz ceremony is performed just prior to

    a.  Passover
    b.  Purim
    c.  Chanuka
    d.  Shemini Atzeret

12. Foods are often associated with specific holidays. Which of the following statements is *not* correct?

    a.  Latkes are eaten on Chanuka.
    b.  Honey is eaten on Rosh Hashana.
    c.  Blintzes are eaten on Purim.
    d.  Herring is eaten on Tisha B'Av.

**13.** The period of intensive mourning for the loss of a loved one is called *Shiva*, a Hebrew word meaning

    a. sitting
    b. sadness
    c. seven
    d. thirty

**14.** Traditionally, three meals are eaten on the Sabbath. The third meal is known by the Hebrew name

    a. shalosh regalim
    b. Shabbat shalom
    c. shalachmones
    d. se'uda shelishit

**15.** One of the Five Scrolls (Megillot) is the Book of Ruth, which tells the story of a Moabite girl who embraced Judaism. On which holiday is it read in the synagogue, and why?

    a. on Passover, because it is the holiday when the Jews won their freedom
    b. on Shavuot, because it is the holiday on which the Jews accepted the Torah
    c. on Chanuka, because it is the holiday on which a tyrant was defeated
    d. on Sukkot, beacuse it is an agricultural holiday

**16.** The etrog and lulav are used on the Sukkot holiday. An etrog is a citron. What is a lulav?

    a. a willow branch
    b. a myrtle branch
    c. a palm branch
    d. an olive branch

17. The special dessert that is served as the last food at the Passover Seder meal is called

    a. charoset
    b. afikomon
    c. maror
    d. karpas

18. Tisha B'Av, which commemorates the destruction of the First and Second Temples, has much in common with two of the following holidays because of the manner in which they are observed. Which two?

    a. Passover
    b. Purim
    c. Yom Kippur
    d. Asara B'Tevet

19. The three major festivals—Pesach (Passover), Shavuot (Pentecost), and Sukkot (Tabernacles)—are called the

    a. Pilgrim Festivals
    b. High Holidays
    c. Shemini Atzeret
    d. Chol Ha-moed

20. The Book of Lamentations is read in the synagogue on

    a. Yom Kippur
    b. Purim
    c. Tisha B'Av
    d. Shavuot

21. Rosh Hashana is the Jewish New Year. Another Jewish holiday is referred to as the New Year for Trees. What is the Hebrew name of this holiday and when does it occur in the Jewish calendar?

    a. Sukkot—the fifteenth day of Tishri
    b. Tisha B'Av—the ninth day of Av
    c. Chamisha Asar Bi-Shevat—the fifteenth day of Shevat
    d. Asara B'Tevet—the tenth day of Tevet

22. In observant Jewish homes the fire on the stove is kept burning throughout the Sabbath. A metal covering is placed over the flame. This covering is called a

    a. mantle
    b. bima
    c. breastplate
    d. blech

23. In chapter 11 of the Book of Leviticus, certain types of animals are described as kosher (ritually fit to eat), and certain ones are described as not kosher. The main characteristics of a kosher animal are that it

    a. has split hooves and smooth skin
    b. chews the cud and has split hooves
    c. chews the cud and has smooth skin
    d. chews the cud and has at least one split hoof

24. More wine is drunk on one particular holiday than on all others. Which is it?

    a. Passover
    b. Purim
    c. Chanuka
    d. Rosh Hashana

25. Yizkor is a Hebrew prayer for the dead recited in most synagogues on three festivals and on the Day of Atonement. Which are the three festivals?

   a. Rosh Hashana, Passover, Sukkot
   b. Pesach, Shavuot, Rosh Hashana
   c. Passover, Sukkot, Shavuot
   d. Passover, Shavuot, Shemini Atzeret

26. Which of these holidays fall in the same Hebrew month?

   a. Rosh Hashana
   b. Yom Kippur
   c. Sukkot
   d. Purim

27. Wine plays an important role in Jewish life, but two groups mentioned in the Bible refrained from drinking wine. Who are they?

   a. Nazirites and Rechabites
   b. Pharisees and Sadducees
   c. Ashkenazim and Sephardim
   d. Shammaites and Hillelites

28. The number of people given aliyot during a Torah reading is not always the same. On Sabbaths, seven aliyot are distributed, but on major holidays that fall on a weekday only

   a. three are awarded
   b. four are awarded
   c. five are awarded
   d. six are awarded

**29.** Bikur cholim is one of the most important commandments in Judaism. It means

    a. burying the dead
    b. honoring one's father and mother
    c. visiting the sick
    d. paying a condolence call

**30.** The first day of the Ten Days of Repentance is

    a. Rosh Hashana
    b. Yom Kippur
    c. Tisha B'Av
    d. Sukkot

**31.** Most Jewish holidays are described for the first time in the Book of Leviticus. Which one of the following holidays is not mentioned in the Bible at all?

    a. Tabernacles
    b. Chanuka
    c. Pentecost
    d. Purim

**32.** In the English calendar, when a leap year occurs every four years, one day is added to February, making it twenty-nine days long. When leap years occur in the Jewish calendar

    a. two days are added to the month of Tishri
    b. a whole month, called Adar II, is added to the calendar year
    c. one day is added to the month of Adar
    d. one day is subtracted from the month Sivan

33.  Of the major holidays mentioned in the Bible, which two begin on the fifteenth day of the month?

  a.  Rosh Hashana and Yom Kippur
  b.  Purim and Chanuka
  c.  Passover and Sukkot
  d.  Shavuot and Purim

34.  The Book of Leviticus (25:8-17) declares that at the end of seven sabbatical years, the fiftieth year is to be observed as a jubilee year. In that year

  a.  liberty was proclaimed throughout the land to all the inhabitants
  b.  the land was to lie fallow
  c.  all land was to be restored to the original owners
  d.  all slaves were to be set free

35.  In chapter 11 of the Book of Leviticus, certain types of fish are described as kosher and others as not kosher. A fish is kosher if it

  a.  has fins
  b.  has scales
  c.  has both fins and scales
  d.  is slaughtered by a shochet

36.  At the end of a wedding ceremony, the bridegroom breaks a glass. It is generally said that this act is performed as a

  a.  reminder of the destruction of the Temple
  b.  symbol of the breaking of the groom's ties with his family
  c.  reminder that one's cup of life can never be full
  d.  indication that the ceremony has concluded

37. Of the three Pilgrim Festivals, one is called Sukkot in Hebrew. Its English name is

    a. Pentecost
    b. Apocrypha
    c. Tabernacles
    d. Day of Atonement

38. After the Jews were saved from Haman's plot of annihilation, all Jews were urged to celebrate by sending gifts to friends and to the poor. This activity is known in Hebrew as

    a. mishloach manot
    b. Purim
    c. chad gadya
    d. pidyon ha-ben

39. The document that a groom gives his bride at a wedding ceremony, and which must be attested to by two witnesses is called a

    a. ketuba
    b. get
    c. prosbul
    d. kedusha

40. A girl can become a Bat Mitzva at a younger age than a boy becomes a Bar Mitzva. A boy must be thirteen years of age and a girl must be at least

    a. ten years of age
    b. eleven years of age
    c. twelve years of age
    d. eleven and one-half years of age

**41.** The circumcision ceremony, known as the *Brit*, is performed on the

    a. sixth day after the birth of a boy
    b. seventh day after the birth of a boy
    c. eighth day after the birth of a boy
    d. ninth day after the birth of a boy

**42.** The wire or rope that is strung around the perimeter of a community so as to convert it legally from a public to a private domain is called

    a. aguna
    b. eruv
    c. kvitl
    d. prosbul

**43.** The Priestly Benediction is called *Birkat Kohanim* in Hebrew, and the ceremony in which it is recited is popularly known as *duchening*. The ceremony is so called because when the blessings are recited the Priests

    a. cover their heads
    b. stand on their toes
    c. stand on a platform
    d. bend their knees

**44.** *Halacha* (also spelled *halakhah*) is derived from the Hebrew verb *haloch*, meaning "go" or "walk." It refers to the

    a. way a Jew must conduct his life
    b. path leading to Jerusalem
    c. streets of the Old City of Jerusalem
    d. dietary laws

**45.** The dreidel has been used for many years to play a game on Chanuka. Four different Hebrew letters appear on the sides of the dreidel. One is *nun;* another is *gimmel;* a third is *hay.* What is the fourth letter?

    a. dalet
    b. aleph
    c. shin
    d. bet

**46.** A minyan, or quorum, traditionally required in order to hold a full religious service, must include the presence of

    a. ten males or females over age twenty-one
    b. ten males over age thirteen
    c. ten males or females over age twelve
    d. ten people of any age

**47.** A man and his ten sons were put to death on a day which became the holiday of

    a. Chanuka
    b. Purim
    c. Lag B'Omer
    d. Tisha B'Av

**48.** After congregants have paraded around the synagogue on Hoshana Rabba, the last day of Sukkot, each congregant beats an object against the back of a pew or on the floor. The object is a

    a. bunch of willows
    b. citron
    c. palm branch
    d. myrtle branch

**49.** Dishes filled with salt water are placed on the Seder table. During the course of the Seder service, participants dip two of the following foods into the salt water. They are

   a. horseradish
   b. vegetable
   c. hard-boiled egg
   d. matza

**50.** Lag B'Omer is a minor holiday on which, according to tradition, a plague that took the lives of many students of Rabbi Akiba (second century) ended. During what season of the year is Lag B'Omer celebrated?

   a. winter
   b. spring
   c. summer
   d. autumn

**51.** The word *Shaddai* (God) appears prominently on one of the ceremonial objects used by Jews. That object is the

   a. mezuza
   b. kiddush cup
   c. breastplate
   d. talit

**52.** A famous first-century rabbi created a sandwich that is eaten at every Seder. It consists of two pieces of matza with

   a. horseradish between them
   b. charoset between them
   c. egg between them
   d. cucumber between them

**53.** Several Jewish holidays came into being after World War II. Two of them are

    a. Tu Bi-Shevat
    b. Simchat Torah
    c. Yom Yerushala'yim
    d. Yom Ha-atzma'ut

**54.** The terms "nine days" and "three weeks" apply to a period of time during the summer months when

    a. weddings are traditionally prohibited
    b. Bar Mitzvas are not held
    c. Bat Mitzvas are not held
    d. bread and wine are not eaten

**55.** At a circumcision, the man and woman who serve as godfather and godmother are called

    a. kvater and kvaterin
    b. chossen and kalla
    c. shabbos and yontif
    d. gog and magog

**56.** There is no such person as a half-Jew because according to Jewish law the only person who can be called a Jew is one

    a. whose father is a Jew
    b. whose mother is a Jew
    c. whose grandfather is a Jew
    d. who was converted to Judaism

**57.** Which of the following sets of three objects is associated with the same holiday?

    a. matza, lulav, etrog
    b. lulav, etrog, sukka
    c. dreidel, menora, mezuza
    d. aravot, lulav, lekach

58. On which two holidays does an observant Jew avoid eating and drinking for at least twenty-four hours?

    a. Yom Kippur and Asara B'Tevet
    b. Yom Kippur and Tzom Gedaliah
    c. Yom Kippur and Taanit Esther
    d. Yom Kippur and Tisha B'Av

59. The anniversary of the death of a close relative is observed by kindling a memorial candle and reciting the Kaddish. The observance is known as

    a. Yahrzeit
    b. Matzeva
    c. Yizkor
    d. Shiva

60. On the day before the Yom Kippur holiday, it was once quite common to wave a rooster (for men) or a hen (for women) over one's head and to designate it as a symbol of atonement for one's sins. The custom is called

    a. kabtzan
    b. kabbala
    c. kapparot
    d. kamaya

61. The special prayer recited at mealtime on Sabbaths and holidays which recalls the act of Creation is called

    a. Kiddush
    b. Kaddish
    c. Karpas
    d. Ha-motzi

62. The act of making a tear in the outer garment of a mourner is called

    a. halacha
    b. kaddish
    c. keria
    d. kabbala

63. Rosh Hashana occurs on the first day of the Hebrew month of

    a. Tishri
    b. Elul
    c. Nissan
    d. Sivan

64. The meat of an animal such as a cow or a sheep is kosher. According to the dietary laws, it can be consumed only if it is

    a. properly slaughtered, salted, and rinsed
    b. properly slaughtered and salted
    c. properly slaughtered and rinsed
    d. properly slaughtered, salted, and boiled

65. Which of these songs is sung at the Passover Seder?

    a. "Adon Olam"
    b. "Chad Gadya"
    c. "Maoz Tzur"
    d. "Shalom Alechem"

66. *Ya'aleh ve-yavo* are the first words of a prayer recited as part of the Amida and Grace After Meals on certain days. These days are

    a. Rosh Hashana and Yom Kippur
    b. Rosh Chodesh and pilgrimage festivals
    c. Chanukah and Purim
    d. Rosh Hashana and Sukkot

**67.** The Kol Nidre prayer is recited on

    a. Rosh Hashana
    b. Yom Kippur
    c. Rosh Hashana and Yom Kippur
    d. Yom Kippur and Sukkot

**68.** Many traditional Jews beat their breasts when reciting the Yom Kippur prayer that begins with the words

    a. shema Yisrael
    b. adon olam
    c. al chet
    d. shema kolaynu

**69.** The shofar that is used on Rosh Hashana is a ram's horn. The horn of a ram rather than that of another animal was selected because Abraham found a ram to use as a substitute when he was about to

    a. sacrifice his son Isaac
    b. sacrifice his son Ishmael
    c. circumcise his son Esau
    d. prepare a meal for his family

**70.** A favorite treat enjoyed on the Chamisha Asar Bi-Shevat holiday is

    a. bokser
    b. cholent
    c. latkes
    d. knaidlach

**71.** With which holiday are the following words associated: hadasim, aravot, s'chach, and pitom?

    a. Yom Kippur
    b. Purim
    c. Sukkot
    d. Shavuot

**72.** One of the popular sections of the Passover Haggadah is written in a style similar to the poem "The House That Jack Built." It was composed in the fifteenth century. The name of the selection is

    a. Adon Olam
    b. Chad Gadya
    c. Ma Nishtana
    d. Hallel

**73.** A very popular food usually served at the Sabbath afternoon light meal is

    a. latkes
    b. hamantaschen
    c. chopped liver
    d. herring

**74.** During the reading of the Megilla on Purim, whenever the name of Haman is mentioned, it is customary to make noise. The instrument usually used for this purpose is called a

    a. dreidel
    b. shofar
    c. grogger
    d. hamantasch

**75.** Before a traditional wedding begins, some rabbis conduct a private ceremony called Kinyan Sudar, which symbolically confirms that a man is "acquiring" a wife. The instrument of the acquisition is a

    a. shoe
    b. talit
    c. mezuza
    d. handkerchief

76. "Maoz Tzur", a well-known Hebrew hymn that was composed in the thirteenth century, is known in English as Rock of Ages. It is sung by Ashkenazic Jews after

   a. eating the afikomon on Passover
   b. eating blintzes on Shavuot
   c. lighting the Chanuka candles
   d. using the lulav on Sukkot

77. According to the Rabbis of the Talmud, even before the Torah and its laws were given on Mount Sinai, a series of laws had been enacted that were binding on all people, Jews and non-Jews. These laws are known as the

   a. Noahide Laws
   b. Abrahamitic Laws
   c. Laws of Hammurabi
   d. Laws of Purity

78. Since biblical law demanded that in every seventh year (the sabbatical year) all debts be canceled, those in financial need were not granted loans as the sabbatical year approached. To remedy this situation, Hillel introduced a concept called

   a. aguna
   b. jubilee
   c. prosbul
   d. shemita

# The Language
# of Judaism

4

1.  One Hebrew term for holiday has the literal meaning of "good day." That term is

    a. yom ha-din
    b. yom tov
    c. yom terua
    d. chag

2.  The Arabic word *ibn* and the Aramaic word *bar*, both meaning "son [of]," have the same meaning as the Hebrew word

    a. baal
    b. bat
    c. ben
    d. baruch

3.  *Akshan* is a Hebrew/Yiddish term meaning

    a. stubborn person
    b. philanderer
    c. beggar
    d. marriage counselor

4.  The Hebrew words *Kol Nidre*, *Al Chet*, and *Ashamnu* refer to prayers that are recited during

    a. the circumcision ceremony
    b. the Torah reading
    c. the Yom Kippur service
    d. the Pidyon Ha-ben ceremony

5.  The Hebrew word for charity is *tzedaka*, the literal meaning of which is

    a. pity
    b. righteousness
    c. comfort
    d. kindness

**6.** The accents or musical notes that are chanted by the person reading the Torah are called

    a. chazeret
    b. sidra
    c. neginot
    d. te'amim

**7.** *Arba kanfot*, meaning "four corners," is the name of a small undergarment with fringes on its four corners. It is also called

    a. atara
    b. kipa
    c. talit katan
    d. tagin

**8.** Adoshem and Adonai are names that refer to

    a. holiday delicacies
    b. God
    c. Jewish prophets
    d. the High Priests of Israel

**9.** Abbreviations and acronyms are very common in Hebrew. Which of these is the Hebrew acronym for Bible, and what are the three words for which it stands?

    a. Rashi
    b. Tanach
    c. Rambam
    d. Mishna

**10.** If a woman's husband has disappeared and it cannot be determined whether he is living or dead, the woman is not permitted to remarry. She is called

    a. kallah
    b. chalitza
    c. aguna
    d. eshet cha'yil

**11.** The Hebrew expression meaning "with God's help" is

    a. kiddush Ha-Shem
    b. mazal tov
    c. siman tov
    d. b'ezrat Ha-Shem

**12.** Adon Olam is the name of

    a. a popular Israeli general
    b. a popular prayer
    c. a Sephardic-Jewish politician
    d. the president of Hebrew University

**13.** The Hebrew word meaning "to go up" or "ascend" is used to describe the honor bestowed upon a person called to recite the blessings over the Torah. The word is

    a. aliya
    b. beracha
    c. kaddish
    d. mitzva

**14.** *Sheva Berachot* means "seven blessings." They are recited as the concluding prayers at a marriage ceremony but they are also recited by traditional Jews

    a. at Sabbath meals after a circumcision
    b. for seven weeks after a couple is engaged
    c. at a daily festive meal for seven days after a wedding
    d. after a Pidyon Ha-ben

**15.** Which of the following words have a direct connection with the Talmud?

    a. Yerushalmi
    b. Bavli
    c. Essene
    d. Pharisee

**16.** The pointer used by a Torah reader is known in Hebrew as a *yad* because it is shaped like a

    a. hand
    b. rod
    c. finger
    d. shofar

**17.** A person who is a descendant of a family of distinction is said to have

    a. yichus
    b. yahrzeit
    c. tashlich
    d. tayglach

**18.** The *shekel*, the *peruta*, and the *agora* have been used in both ancient and modern Israel. These are

    a. measures of weight
    b. types of coins
    c. types of food
    d. names of books

**19.** The Haggadah, the Machzor, and the Siddur have one thing in common. They are types of

    a. Bibles
    b. foods
    c. prayerbooks
    d. ritual garments

**20.** Which of the following terms refers to a food that has sour grass as its major ingredient?

    a. s'chav
    b. borsht
    c. cholent
    d. chamin

21. The term for a native Israeli is the same as the Arabic word for a prickly pear or cactus. The term was adopted because this type of plant is supposed to characterize a person with a tough exterior and a tender interior. The Arabic word is

    a. Yisraeli
    b. Sabra
    c. Yehudi
    d. Allah

22. A Jewish woman who is a good housekeeper is called a

    a. badchan
    b. balabusta
    c. kvaterin
    d. baalat tefila

23. The words Machzor, Piyyut, and Amida are all connected with

    a. Jewish philosophy
    b. Jewish art
    c. Jewish liturgy
    d. designs of synagogue

24. The Judeo-Spanish dialect spoken by Sephardim of the Mediterranean area is called

    a. Yiddish
    b. Ladino
    c. Esperanto
    d. Marrano

**25.** Daggerlike ornamental strokes that look like crowns appear on some of the letters in handwritten copies of the Torah. They are called

a. tagin
b. masora
c. trop
d. aravot

**26.** When one says "once in a *shmita*," he or she means

a. once a year
b. once a month
c. once in a long time
d. once in fifty years

**27.** The English alphabet consists of twenty-six letters. How many letters are there in the Hebrew alphabet?

a. twenty-two including five final letters
b. twenty-seven plus five final letters
c. twenty-two plus five final letters
d. twenty-seven, the same as the English alphabet

**28.** Although the Hebrew phrase *am ha-aretz* literally means "people of the land," the colloquial meaning is

a. real estate investor
b. ignoramus
c. Zionist
d. wise person

**29.** Shacharit, Mincha, and Maariv are the names of

a. Israeli newspapers
b. prayer services
c. Israeli dances
d. political parties in the Knesset

**30.** A Jew who does not believe in God is called

    a. meshumad
    b. apikores
    c. akshan
    d. batlan

**31.** The Yiddish expression *biz hundert und tzvansig* means "[may you live] until one hundred and twenty." The number was selected because according to tradition one man in the Bible lived to be that age. His name is

    a. Aaron
    b. Isaac
    c. Abraham
    d. Moses

**32.** One of the names of the twelve Hebrew months means "father." Which is it?

    a. Elul
    b. Av
    c. Adar
    d. Tammuz

**33.** The opposite of *mitzva* is

    a. avera
    b. etrog
    c. minyan
    d. lulav

**34.** A baal koray is a person who is expert at

    a. ritual slaughtering
    b. reading the Torah
    c. building synagogues
    d. blowing a shofar

**35.** The person who leads a congregation in prayer is called by several names. Which of these is the correct name?

    a.  baal tefila
    b.  chazzan
    c.  cantor
    d.  shaliach tzibur

**36.** There are many ways of saying congratulations in Hebrew. Which of the following are *not* congratulatory terms?

    a.  yasher koach
    b.  mazal tov
    c.  lag b'omer
    d.  le-hitra'ot

**37.** Bet ha-kevarot, bet olam, and bet ha-cha'yim are all synonyms for

    a.  synagogue
    b.  cemetery
    c.  house of study
    d.  house of prayer

**38.** In European Jewish communities during the eighteenth and nineteenth centuries, it was common for a particular type of person to provide entertainment at joyous celebrations. The entertainer was called a

    a.  badchan
    b.  shadchan
    c.  mohel
    d.  chazzan

**39.** The first word of every blessing begins with a Hebrew word meaning "blessed." That word is

  a. beracha
  b. baruch
  c. shema
  d. adon

**40.** A person who is lazy and wastes time is called a

  a. shadchan
  b. batlan
  c. kabtzan
  d. chazzan

**41.** The home ceremony marking the end of the Sabbath consists of the recitation of special prayers over a cup of wine at which time spices and a candle are used. The Hebrew word for the ceremony is

  a. Havdala
  b. Besamim
  c. Shabbat
  d. Kiddush

**42.** The Hebrew expressions *Biur Chametz* and *Bedikat Chametz* are associated with ceremonies relating to the holiday of

  a. Passover
  b. Shavuot
  c. Yom Kippur
  d. Chanukah

**43.** The lamp that burns continuously in every synagogue is called

    a. havdala
    b. yahrzeit
    c. ner tamid
    d. menora

**44.** Mah Tovu, Sim Shalom, Alenu, and Sholom Alechem are the names of

    a. Hebrew novels
    b. prayers
    c. Jewish authors.
    d. Israeli cities

**45.** *Nachas*, a Yiddish expression of Hebrew origin, means

    a. pain and privation
    b. poverty and sickness
    c. peace, pleasure, contentment
    d. wealth and prosperity

**46.** The popular Hebrew greeting *chag same'ach* is generally exchanged

    a. at funerals
    b. at unveilings
    c. on holidays
    d. on Sabbaths

**47.** The combined numerical value of the two Hebrew letters that make up the word *chai* is

    a. one hundred
    b. thirty-six
    c. twenty-six
    d. eighteen

**48.** The words *shtreimel*, *sheitel*, *gartle*, and *kipa* refer to

    a. types of food
    b. articles that are worn
    c. types of literature
    d. Torah ornaments

**49.** The biblical ceremony that is performed when a man refuses to marry his brother's childless widow is called

    a. Ha-motzi
    b. Chalitza
    c. Hallel
    d. Yibum

**50.** During the marriage ceremony, the bride and groom stand under a canopy while the ceremony is conducted. The Hebrew word for canopy is

    a. chupa
    b. ketuba
    c. kalla
    d. gartl

**51.** Of the six congratulatory expressions used by Jews, which of the following are used primarily by Ashkenazim?

    a. mazal u-veracha
    b. be-siman tov
    c. ye-yasher kochacha
    d. chazak u-varuch
    e. tizkeh le-mitzvot
    f. mazal tov

**52.** The Israeli airline, established in 1949, now carries passengers and freight worldwide. It is named El Al, two Hebrew words that mean

    a. all for one
    b. for everybody
    c. on high
    d. everyman's airline

**53.** Of these, the prayer that is always recited at funeral services is

    a. Adon Olam
    b. El Malay Rachamim
    c. Chad Gadya
    d. Yigdal

**54.** In every Jewish home, a mezuza is mounted on

    a. the upper third of the right doorpost, as one enters
    b. the upper section of the right doorpost, as one leaves
    c. any part of the doorpost, on either side
    d. the upper third of the left doorpost, as one enters

**55.** The confession of sins is a prominent feature of Jewish liturgy, particularly on the Day of Atonement. The best known example is the Al Chet prayer, which is an enumeration of various types of sins. The general Hebrew term for confession of sins is

    a. Kiddush
    b. Viddui
    c. Kaddish
    d. Machzor

**56.** A Hebrew phrase meaning "profanation of the Name [of God]," refers to any action by a Jew that would bring disgrace upon Jews or Judaism. The actual Hebrew phrase is

    a. kiddush Ha-Shem
    b. chillul Ha-Shem
    c. sholom Aleichem
    d. baruch Ha-Shem

**57.** The person in charge of certifying that food is kosher is called a

    a. mashgiach
    b. mashiach
    c. shaliach
    d. gabbai

**58.** Cholent, chremzel, gehakte leber, gribenes, kichlach, and tayglach are all types of Jewish

    a. ceremonies
    b. foods
    c. ritual garments
    d. chassidic garb

**59.** The Yiddish word *shaleshudis* is a distorted form of the Hebrew words

    a. shalosh regalim
    b. shelosha avot
    c. shalosh se'udot
    d. shalom yehudi

**60.** The Yiddish word *frum* means

    a. charitable person
    b. compassionate person
    c. pious person
    d. stranger

**61.** A synagogue official who is appointed to supervise the awarding of Torah honors (aliyot), escort worshippers to their seats, or supervise the decorum is called a

    a. chazzan
    b. gabbai
    c. baal koray
    d. baal tefila

**62.** Although automation is a recent innovation, the idea of an automaton in human form dates back to talmudic days. Stories of such a creature recur in Jewish literature up to the sixteenth century. What is this automaton called in Hebrew?

    a. golem
    b. galut
    c. gedula
    d. mashiach
    e. shammes

**63.** A Hebrew expression meaning "of blessed memory," sometimes used when speaking of a deceased person, is

    a. zichrono li-veracha
    b. le-cha'yim
    c. le-hitra'ot
    d. alav ha-shalom

**64.** A long, narrow band of material is used to tie together a Torah scroll. Sometimes this sash is made of swaddling cloths that were used at a boy's circumcision. It is called a

    a. kvitl
    b. gartle
    c. kipa
    d. talit

**65.** One of the following terms is occasionally used as a synonym for God. That word is

    a. Shechita
    b. Shmita
    c. Shechina
    d. Darshan

**66.** In talmudic times (basically the first five centuries of the present era) teachers delivered their lectures through an interpreter. The lecturer would speak in a soft voice, and the interpreter would repeat the utterances in a loud voice. The interpreter was called a(n)

    a. tanna
    b. amora
    c. meturgeman
    d. batlan

**67.** A lively Israeli folk dance performed in a circle has its origin in Rumania and Turkey. The dance, which took root in Palestine after World War I, is called the

    a. twist
    b. havdala
    c. hatikva
    d. hora

**68.** The following three Hebrew words and phrases have the same general meaning: *yamim tovim*, *chaggim*, and *mo'adim*. They all refer to

    a. holidays
    b. fast days
    c. birthdays
    d. national celebrations

**69.** *Im yirtzeh Ha-Shem* is a Hebrew phrase meaning

    a. if it pleases God
    b. happy holiday
    c. till we meet again
    d. praise be to God

**70.** The prayer recited by mourners is called

    a. Korban
    b. Kaddish
    c. Kedusha
    d. Maariv

**71.** When taking leave of someone, the Hebrew phrase used is

    a. le-cha'yim
    b. le-hitra'ot
    c. mazal tov
    d. shalom alechem

**72.** About two thousand years ago, Jews established a correct way of spelling and pronouncing the Hebrew text of the Bible. This tradition became known as the

    a. Pentateuch
    b. Mishna
    c. Masora
    d. Septuagint

**73.** A pudding (usually round) made of noodles or potatoes, traditionally served on Sabbaths and holidays, is known as

    a. kugel
    b. shnapps
    c. kichel
    d. kashe

**74.** The Yiddish word for a person who mixes into other people's business is

    a. kashe
    b. knishes
    c. kochleffl
    d. knaydl

**75.** According to talmudic legend, it is through the merit of thirty-six saintly persons that the world continues to exist. A person who is a member of this group is a

    a. lamdan
    b. kabtzan
    c. shadchan
    d. lamed vovnik

**76.** The word *lekach* refers to a special type of cake. This delicacy is a

    a. nut cake
    b. honey cake
    c. cheese cake
    d. layer cake

**77.** *Minhag Ashkenaz*, *Minhag Polin*, and *Minhag Sefarad* refer to various types of

    a. ritual practices
    b. institutions of learning
    c. charitable institutions
    d. prayer practices

**78.** A biblical word meaning "lightheaded person" has become a popular Yiddish term for a person who is always clowning. The word is

    a. letz
    b. loksch
    c. luftmensch
    d. lamdan

**79.** The name of God in Hebrew is treated with special sanctity. Therefore, instead of writing out the full name of God, some of the following letters are used in its place as an abbreviated form. They are

  a. alef
  b. dalet
  c. yud
  d. hay

**80.** In 1916 Max Nordau, a Budapest-born Zionist leader coined a German expression that describes a type of Jew who lived in Eastern Europe. This Jew was without a stable occupation and lived on peddling and petty speculation. The term he used was

  a. Luftmenschen
  b. Chassidim
  c. Hofjuden
  d. Mitnagdim

**81.** The Yiddish word for headcovering is *yarmulke*. The Hebrew equivalent is

  a. kitl
  b. koppel
  c. kvitl
  d. kipa

**82.** In pre-state years, the entire Jewish community in Palestine was referred to as the

  a. knesset
  b. yeshiva
  c. yishuv
  d. kibbutz

**83.** Every blessing uttered in Hebrew begins with the
words

    a. baruch ha-Shem
    b. Shema Yisrael
    c. baruch ata
    d. baruch ha-ba

**84.** An itinerant East European musician was known as

    a. chazzan
    b. klezmer
    c. baal teshuva
    d. baal Keria

# Great Personalities 5

1.  Henry Kissinger, Menachem Begin, and Albert H. Fried were all

    a. prime ministers
    b. recipients of the Nobel Prize for Peace
    c. advisors to presidents
    d. professors

2.  Benjamin Nathan Cardozo was the second Jew to be appointed to a very high office by a president of the United States. In 1932 he was chosen to succeed Oliver Wendell Homes as

    a. Supreme Court justice
    b. Court of Appeals judge
    c. attorney general of the U.S.
    d. ambassador to Spain

3.  Louis Buchalter, Arnold Rothstein, Benjamin Siegel, and Meyer Lansky were well-known

    a. politicians
    b. philanthropists
    c. criminals
    d. criminologists

4.  An English financier and moneylender who died in 1185 had among his clients members of the nobility as well as religious leaders. He provided funds to Christians, enabling them to build abbeys and cathedrals. Upon his death, the Crown confiscated all of his property. His name is

    a. Benjamin Disraeli
    b. Louis Dembitz Brandeis
    c. Aaron of Lincoln
    d. Baron Edmond de Rothschild

**5.** Many famous Jews were named Adler. One of these was a great psychologist, one a great journalist, one a rabbi, and one a scholar and community leader. The scholar who became the president of a seminary is

    a. Alfred Adler
    b. Julius Ochs Adler
    c. Cyrus Adler
    d. Nathan Marcus Adler

**6.** According to legend, a simple uneducated man who was born in Palestine about 40 C.E. left his wife and went off to begin his studies at the age of forty. His wife's name was Rachel and his father-in-law's name was Kalba Sabua. What was his name?

    a. Akiba ben Joseph
    b. Judah the Prince
    c. Hillel the Elder
    d. Elisha ben Avuya

**7.** These men have occupied high political office in their respective states. Which two served as governor?

    a. Jacob Javits of New York
    b. Moses Alexander of Idaho
    c. Arthur Seligman of New Mexico
    d. Edward Koch of New York

**8.** According to legend, the king of Macedonia visited Jerusalem during his reign (336-323 B.C.E.). He was very friendly toward Jews. As a token of appreciation, many Jews named sons born in that year after him. What is the monarch's name?

    a. Josephus
    b. Aristotle
    c. Alexander
    d. Cyrus

9.　Jewish scholars who lived in Palestine and Babylonia from the third century to the sixth century C.E. and whose opinions are recorded in the second part of the Talmud are called

    a.　Amoraim
    b.　Pharisees
    c.　Tosafists
    d.　Karaites

10.　The father of modern chassidism, Israel ben Eliezer of the Ukraine (1700-1760), is more popularly known as the

    a.　Baal Tefila
    b.　Baal Brit
    c.　Baal Shem Tov
    d.　Baal Keria

11.　Born in 1870, this man was an important financier and public official. He was especially known as an advisor on economic matters to many U. S. presidents. His name is

    a.　Billy Rose
    b.　Arthur Goldberg
    c.　Bernard Baruch
    d.　Edmond Rothschild

12.　This twelfth-century Spanish Jewish world traveler visited 300 different Jewish communities in his lifetime and wrote a book about his travels. His name is

    a.　Benjamin of Tudela
    b.　Benjamin of Bachrach
    c.　Moses Maimonides
    d.　Moses ben Nachman

**13.** A French Jew born in 1907 held many appointed and elective offices in France between 1932 (when he was elected to the French parliament) and 1956 (when he served as vice premier under Mollet). From June 1954 to February 1955 he served as premier of France. His name is

    a. Pierre Mendés-France
    b. Henri Louis Bergson
    c. Jean Benoit-Lévy
    d. Alfred Dreyfus

**14.** This brilliant wife of Rabbi Meir, a leading second-century talmudic scholar, is the only woman mentioned in the Talmud as having participated in legal discussions. Her two children died on the same day, on a Sabbath, but she kept the fact from her husband until after the Sabbath. What was her name?

    a. Alexandra
    b. Beruria
    c. Rachel
    d. Deborah

**15.** Léon Blum, who started his career as a literary critic and author, became involved in the socialist movement in France. The high point of his career was becoming

    a. premier of France in the Popular Front Government
    b. a Nobel Prize winner for his literary achievements
    c. chairman of the board of the Jewish Agency
    d. head of the French Communist Party

16. This philosopher, born in 1878, was a professor at the Hebrew University. He emerged as one of the greatest authorities on chassidism and had a great influence on the Christian world. He conceived of religious faith as a dialogue between man and God. His name is

    a. Franz Rosenzweig
    b. Franz Werfel
    c. Martin Buber
    d. Franz Kafka

17. Many prominent Jews carry the surname Bloch. Perhaps the most celebrated is a Swiss-born composer whose operas include *Macbeth* and *Jezebel*. His first name is

    a. Felix
    b. Ernest
    c. Ivan
    d. Joshua

18. Two of these women had the same first name. Who are they?

    a. Lazarus
    b. Senesz
    c. Abzug
    d. Arendt

19. Two of these men had the same first name. Who are they?

    a. Hess
    b. Mendelsohnn
    c. Herzl
    d. Freud

**20.** Jonas E. Salk, born in 1914, was professor of bacteriology at the University of Pittsburgh from 1949 to 1961. After 1961 he headed the Institute for Biological Research at the University of California. He was awarded the Nobel Prize for his 1955 discovery of a vaccine against

a. diabetes
b. polio
c. measles
d. tuberculosis

**21.** Milton Friedman, Robert J. Samuelson, and Paul Samuelson were outstanding leaders in the field of

a. geology
b. meteorology
c. biology
d. economics

**22.** Chelm (also spelled Helm) is a Polish town whose Jewish settlement dates back to the fifteenth century. The Jewish residents of the town figure in many anecdotes in which they are characterized as

a. wise
b. stingy
c. naive
d. generous

**23.** A personality in the talmudic literature of the first century C.E. who is often called the "Jewish Rip Van Winkle" is said to have slept for seventy years. He is also famous for having drawn a circle around himself, then praying for rain and not leaving the circle until his prayers were answered. This person's name is

  a. Elisha ben Avuyah
  b. Choni Ha-me'aggel
  c. Akiba ben Joseph
  d. Kamtza bar Kamtza

**24.** The Earl of Beaconsfield was a British statesman who was born of Jewish parents in 1804. When he was thirteen, his father had him baptized. From 1874 to 1880 he served as prime minister of England. His name is

  a. Alfred Dreyfus
  b. Benjamin Disraeli
  c. Lord Arthur Balfour
  d. Jacob Barsimon

**25.** In June 1968, after Earl Warren announced his intention to resign as Chief Justice of the U.S. Supreme Court, President Lyndon Johnson proposed elevating Associate Justice Abe Fortas to that post. In October Johnson withdrew Fortas' name because

  a. Republican and Democratic senators opposed it.
  b. Fortas was planning to settle in Israel.
  c. Fortas was offered a good job in the private sector.
  d. Fortas had a nervous breakdown.

**26.** One of the founders of the American Labor Party and the Jewish Labor Committee was born in Poland in 1892. He came to the United States in 1911. From 1932 to 1966 he was president of the International Ladies' Garment Workers' Union. During most of that time he was also vice president of the American Federation of Labor. His name is

    a. David Dubinsky
    b. David Merrick
    c. Arthur Goldberg
    d. Sol Linowitz

**27.** An Israeli diplomat who was born in Capetown, South Africa, in 1915 was a member of the Jewish Agency delegation to the United Nations in 1947. He also represented Israel at the UN from 1948 to 1959 and was Israeli ambassador to the U.S. from 1950 to 1959. In 1960 he became minister of education and culture in Israel. His name is

    a. Chaim Weizmann
    b. Emanuel Neumann
    c. Abba Eban
    d. Binyamin Netanyahu

**28.** After the death of Chaim Weizmann in 1952, this man was invited to make himself available as a candidate for president of Israel. He refused, preferring to stay on at Princeton University, where he could pursue his studies in physics. His name is

    a. Albert Einstein
    b. Sigmund Freud
    c. Jonas Salk
    d. Abba Hillel Silver

**29.** This famous Dutch girl, born in 1929, kept a diary from 1942 to 1944 while hiding from the Nazis in an Amsterdam, Holland, house. When apprehended, she was sent to her death in the Bergen-Belsen concentration camp. Her name is

    a. Hannah Senesh
    b. Hannah Arendt
    c. Emma Lazarus
    d. Anne Frank

**30.** Born in 1882, this great liberal served as an associate justice of the U.S. Supreme Court from 1939 until 1962. From 1914 to 1939 he was a professor at Harvard Law School. He was actively interested in the Zionist movement as early as 1919. His name is

    a. Stephen S. Wise
    b. Felix Frankfurter
    c. Arthur J. Goldberg
    d. Abe Fortas

**31.** This Viennese professor escaped to England in 1933, fleeing the Nazis. He considered all religion, including Judaism, an irrational manifestation of the human mind that is to be treated like other neuroses. In his book *Moses and Monotheism*, which appeared during the final year of his life, he attempted to prove that Moses was an Egyptian. His name is

    a. Carl Jung
    b. Moses Hess
    c. Sigmund Freud
    d. Erich Fromm

**32.** Many false messiahs appeared on the Jewish scene over the centuries. The one who had the greatest impact on Jewish life was born in Izmir (Smyrna), Turkey, in the middle of the seventeenth century. His name is

    a. Solomon Molcho
    b. Shabbetai Tzevi
    c. Jacob Frank
    d. Löbele Prossnitz

**33.** One of the first Jews to arrive in New Amsterdam (New York) in 1654 was a Levy. He fought for the right of Jews to have full citizenship. His first name is

    a. Aaron
    b. Reuben
    c. Asser
    d. Benjamin

**34.** The president of Hebrew Union College since 1947 (in 1950 it merged with the Jewish Institute of Religion) was Nelson Glueck. Prior to becoming the head of the seminary, he achieved fame as a

    a. great historian of the Civil War period
    b. Bible scholar who discovered the Cairo Geniza
    c. archaeologist who discovered King Solomon's mines at Etzion Geber
    d. scientist who developed a test for tuberculosis

**35.** The United States government has issued four commemorative postage stamps honoring a Jew. The first was issued in 1948 honoring Rabbi Alexander D. Goode, a U.S. military chaplain. The others to be honored in this manner were

    a. Albert Einstein, Elie Wiesel, Sandy Koufax
    b. Hank Greenberg, Woody Allen, Barbra Streisand
    c. Henry Kissinger, Edward Koch, Ruth Bader Ginsburg
    d. Samuel Gompers, Albert Einstein, George Gershwin

**36.** *Hatikva,* the national anthem of Israel, was originally a poem written in Hebrew by a man who during his lifetime (1856-1901) lived in Galicia, Rumania, Turkey, and Palestine. His name is

    a. Chaim Nachman Bialik
    b. Shaul Tchernichovsky
    c. Israel Efros
    d. Naphtali Herz Imber

**37.** A descendant of Hillel the Great, this scholar was known not only as president of the Sanhedrin but also as the individual who spearheaded the process which led to the editing of the Mishna. His name is

    a. Rabbi Gamaliel
    b. Yehuda Ha-Nasi
    c. Yehuda Ha-Levi
    d. Rabbi Akiba

**38.** This Chicago-born (1908) labor leader, the youngest child of a Russian immigrant, served the American government at different times as secretary of labor and U.S. ambassador to the United Nations. His name is

    a. Felix Frankfurter
    b. Arthur J. Goldberg
    c. Abraham A. Ribicoff
    d. Samuel Gompers

**39.** The first foreign-born individual ever to become U.S. secretary of state was

    a. William Rogers
    b. Henry Kissinger
    c. Alexander Haig
    d. James Baker

**40.** As far back as 1918, this Jewish leader of Russian extraction (1880-1940) insisted that Jewish self-defense units must be established in Palestine. He was the organizer of the militant Revisionist Zionist Organization. His name is

    a. Theodor Herzl
    b. Moses Hess
    c. Vladimir Jabotinsky
    d. Menachem Ussishkin

**41.** Which of these people lived first?

    a. Akiba
    b. Rashi
    c. Jonah
    d. Maimonides
    e. Josephus
    f. Hillel

42.  A great Jewish philanthropist who made a fortune in the glove business in Gloversville, New York, was the first Harvard football coach (1881) and the first Jewish collegiate coach. He served as a U.S. congressman from 1898 to 1907. At Harvard he established the chair of Jewish Literature and Philosophy, the first ever to be established at any American university. His name is

   a.  Stephen S. Wise
   b.  Lucius N. Littauer
   c.  Mark Wischnitzer
   d.  Walter S. Salant

43.  During World War II, four heroic chaplains lost their lives when their troopship, the *SS Dorchester*, was sunk. One of the four chaplains was a rabbi by the name of

   a.  Stephen S. Wise
   b.  Isaac Mayer Wise
   c.  Alexander D. Goode
   d.  Abraham Heschel

44.  A famous immunologist, born in Hungary in 1877, discovered the test that is able to determine susceptibility to diphtheria. His name is

   a.  Bela Schick
   b.  Jacob Schiff
   c.  Jonas Salk
   d.  Albert Sabin

**45.** Two men named Lewisohn are well known for their contributions to society. Adolph Lewisohn (1849-1938) was an American philanthropist who donated Lewisohn Stadium to the College of the City of New York. Ludwig Lewisohn (1883-1955) achieved fame as

    a. an atomic scientist
    b. a basketball player
    c. a professor and author
    d. a lawyer

**46.** This prominent American statesman served as a U.S. senator (1949-1957) and as governor of New York (1928-32). He was the first director-general of the United Nations Relief and Rehabilitation Agency (1943-1946). His name is

    a. Jacob K. Javits
    b. Emanuel Celler
    c. Herbert H. Lehman
    d. Abraham Ribicoff

**47.** Rambam is an acronym formed from the Hebrew title and name of the famous twelfth-century Spanish scholar Maimonides. His Hebrew name is

    a. Rabbi Moses ben Moshe
    b. Rabbi Moses ben Maimon
    c. Rabbi Moses ben Munkacz
    d. Rabbi Moses ben Nachman

**48.** A famous United States Army officer who graduated from West Point and served in World War II with distinction went to Palestine in 1948 as military advisor to the Haganah. He was killed in action in Jerusalem during the War for Independence. His name is

    a. Yonatan Netanyahu
    b. David Marcus
    c. Kirk Douglas
    d. Vladimir Jabotinsky

**49.** The Marranos of Spain and Portugal, the Chuetas of Majorca, the Jedid-al-Islam in Persia, and the Neofiti of Southern Italy were known as Crypto-Jews because they

    a. observed Passover two weeks after the regular date
    b. did not observe Yom Kippur as a day of fasting
    c. professed another religion outwardly but practiced Judaism secretly
    d. preserved Jewish manuscripts for later generations

**50.** Golda Meir was born in Russia in 1898 but moved to the United States as a child. In 1921 she settled in Palestine. In 1948 Golda became the first Israeli representative to serve in Russia. Her original name was

    a. Golda Meyers
    b. Golda Meyerson
    c. Golda Myerowitz
    d. Golda Mendelson

**51.** Jacob Frank, David Alroy, Avraham Abulafia, and Solomon Molcho lived in different countries during the Middle Ages. They had one thing in common. All were

    a. great physicians
    b. famous artists
    c. false messiahs
    d. Israeli ambassadors

**52.** Amos, Zechariah, and Rashi are famous names in Jewish history. Two of them are prophets mentioned in the Bible. The other was a

    a. newspaper reporter
    b. musician
    c. Bible commentator
    d. physician

**53.** Abraham Albert Michelson, Isaac Isidore Rabi, and Emilio Segre gained fame for their discoveries in one particular field. Each of these Jews won the Nobel Prize for their achievements in

    a. physics
    b. chemistry
    c. literature
    d. music

**54.** In 1977 this Polish-born man became leader of Israel's Labor Party, only to be defeated that year by the Likud Party, headed by Menachem Begin. In 1993 he orchestrated the peace accord between Israel and the Palestine Liberation Organization. His name is

    a. Yitzhak Shamir
    b. Abba Eban
    c. Shimon Peres
    d. Binyamin Netanyahu

55. Of these personalities, publishers of major magazines or newspapers, one also served as a member of the U.S. Congress. That individual, whose father was Jewish but whose mother was not, is

    a. Katherine Graham
    b. Martin Peretz
    c. Joseph Pulitzer
    d. Arthur Hays Sulzberger

56. Many of the great Jewish scholars of the Middle Ages were known best by their acronyms rather than their actual names. What was the acronym of the famous thirteenth-century Spanish commentator on the Bible and Talmud?

    a. Rambam
    b. Ramban
    c. Rashi
    d. Ralbag

57. An Israeli army officer who served as chief of staff from 1949 to 1952 became Professor of Archaeology at the Hebrew University in 1959. He published books about the Dead Sea Scrolls. His name is

    a. Yigael Yadin
    b. Yalkut Shimoni
    c. Julian Morgenstern
    d. Solomon Schechter

58. A former governor of Connecticut was appointed secretary of health, education and welfare in 1961 by President John F. Kennedy. Later he was elected to the Senate. His name is

    a. Abraham Ribicoff
    b. Jacob Javits
    c. Seymour Halpern
    d. Joseph Lieberman

**59.** This American nuclear expert, born in 1900, was an admiral in the U.S. Navy. He was responsible for the development and launching of the world's first atomic submarine in 1952. His name is

    a. Mickey Marcus
    b. Albert Einstein
    c. Hyman George Rickover
    d. J. Robert Oppenheimer

**60.** A German philosopher, born in 1886 of an assimilated family, was on the verge of embracing Christianity when he had a sudden change of heart as a result of his attendance at an Orthodox Yom Kippur service in 1913. His name is

    a. Franz Werfel
    b. Franz Rosenzweig
    c. Sigmund Freud
    d. Nahum Glatzer

**61.** The first member of the famous Rothschild family was Mayer Amschel Rothschild, born in 1743. He had five sons who established themselves in five European centers. They became famous as

    a. financiers
    b. artists
    c. authors
    d. musicians

**62.** In 1954 Polish-born (1906) Albert Sabin, a researcher in infectious diseases, discovered a live virus vaccine that could replace the polio vaccine developed by Jonas Salk. The difference between the two is that whereas

    a. Salk's was administered by injection, Sabin's was taken orally.
    b. Salk's had to be administered every month, Sabin's was administered annually.
    c. Salk's was effective only on children over age ten, Sabin's was effective on all children.
    d. Salk's was extremely expensive to reproduce, Sabin's was only moderately so.

**63.** This American patriot and financier came to the United States from Poland in 1772 and helped finance the American Revolution. With his own funds, he aided such patriots as Robert Morris, James Madison, and Thomas Jefferson. His name is

    a. Jacob H. Schiff
    b. Baron Edmond de Rothschild
    c. Haym Salomon
    d. Judah Touro

**64.** Two famous Rabbis of early talmudic times who were often in disagreement on matters of Jewish law were

    a. Hillel and Shammai
    b. Akiba and Hillel
    c. Judah the Prince and Shammai
    d. Hillel and Rabbi Meir

**65.** A world-famous seventeenth-century Dutch-born philosopher came from a family of Portuguese Marranos. His unorthodox religious views led to his excommunication in 1656 by the Sephardic Jewish community of Amsterdam, Holland. His name is

    a. Baruch Spinoza
    b. Hasdai Crescas
    c. Joseph Caro
    d. Manasseh ben Israel

**66.** This electrical engineer of German birth (1865) came to the United States in 1889. He taught at Union College in Schenectady, New York, and was for many years chief consulting engineer of the General Electric Co. His name is

    a. Thomas Edison
    b. Lewis Strauss
    c. Charles Steinmetz
    d. Adin Steinsaltz

**67.** One of the outstanding diplomats of the World War II period went to great lengths to save Jews. After saving thousands of people, he was abducted in 1945 by the Soviet intelligence service and was never heard from again. His name is

    a. Willie Brandt
    b. Raoul Wallenberg
    c. Kurt Waldheim
    d. U Thant

**68.** Stern is a popular Jewish surname. Avraham Stern (born 1907), Isaac Stern (born 1920), Otto Stern (born 1888), and William Stern (born 1871) are four famous Sterns who achieved distinction in various fields. Which one was the head of the Stern Gang?

    a. Isaac Stern
    b. Otto Stern
    c. Avraham Stern
    d. William Stern

**69.** This archaeologist was born in Poland in 1889 and settled in Palestine in 1912. He taught at the Hebrew University from 1935 until his death in 1953. In 1947 he realized the importance of the Dead Sea Scrolls and acquired several specimens for the Hebrew University. His name is

    a. Chaim Weizmann
    b. Ben Gurion
    c. Eliezer L. Sukenik
    d. Nahman Avigad

**70.** Over the past one hundred years, many Jewish doctors have done significant pioneering work in medical research and have been responsible for many important discoveries. Who of the following is famous for diagnosing syphilis?

    a. August von Wasserman
    b. Sigmund Freud
    c. Ferdinand Cohn
    d. Jonas Salk

**71.** One Jewish Supreme Court justice resigned from the Court at the request of a president after serving for only four years. His name is

    a. Arthur Goldberg
    b. Benjamin Cardozo
    c. Abe Fortas
    d. Felix Frankfurter

**72.** The hymn known as *Yigdal* was composed in Italy in the thirteenth century. It is based on the Thirteen Articles of Faith proposed a century earlier by a famous Jewish philosopher. His name is

    a. Moses Maimonides
    b. Moses ben Nachman
    c. Moses of Coucy
    d. Rashi

**73.** When the only ex-president of the U.S. was appointed to be Chief Justice of the Supreme Court, a Jewish justice was already a member of the Court. The name of the Jewish justice is

    a. Felix Frankfurter
    b. Abe Fortas
    c. Abraham Goldberg
    d. Louis D. Brandeis

**74.** At a meeting held in Basle, Switzerland, in 1897, which of the following men was elected president of a newly formed Zionist organization?

    a. Arthur J. Goldberg
    b. Stephen S. Wise
    c. Theordor Herzl
    d. Chaim Weizmann

**75.** In the year 539 B.C.E. the great ruler of Persia entered Jewish history when he conquered the Babylonian Empire. All Jews living there in exile became subjects of this kindly king whose name is

    a. Nebuchadnezzar
    b. Cyrus
    c. Aristobulus
    d. Herod

**76.** Lee Harvey Oswald, the man who assassinated President John F. Kennedy on November 22, 1963, was killed by a Dallas, Texas, nightclub owner named

    a. Jack Carter
    b. Jack Ruby
    c. George Hart
    d. Frank Cohen

**77.** Lord Arthur James Balfour (1848-1930) was the British foreign secretary who, on November 2, 1917, issued the famous Balfour Declaration, which stated that

    a. Arabs and Jews should share Palestine
    b. Palestine should become a Jewish homeland
    c. Arabs should have Palestine as a homeland
    d. Jews should be given a homeland in Africa

**78.** This man is said to be the first Jewish settler to arrive in New Amsterdam (New York). He is believed to have arrived at least one month before Jews from Brazil in 1654. What is his name?

    a. Salo Baron
    b. Jacob Barsimon
    c. Judah Touro
    d. Uriah Phillips

**79.** The first president of the State of Israel was Chaim Weizmann, a chemist by profession. Yitzhak Ben-Zvi was the second president. In addition to his involvement in politics, Ben-Zvi gained a reputation as a

    a. journalist and scholar
    b. doctor of medicine
    c. farmer
    d. physicist

**80.** This Swedish diplomat, born in 1895, negotiated with the Germans at the end of World War II to rescue Jewish survivors. He was assassinated in Jerusalem in 1948 while serving as a United Nations mediator in the Jewish-Arab conflict. His name is

    a. Count Folke Bernadotte
    b. Dag Hammarskjold
    c. Arthur Balfour
    d. Adolph Eichmann

**81.** The minister of defense during Israel's 1967 Six-Day War and 1973 Yom Kippur War was a general named

    a. Motta Gur
    b. Chaim Herzog
    c. Ezer Weizman
    d. Moshe Dayan

**82.** Georges Clemenceau (1841-1929), the great French statesman, was a leading defender of a Jewish French army captain accused of betraying France. Clemenceau edited the journal in which Émile Zola's famous article *J'accuse!* first appeared. What was the name of the Jewish captain who was falsely accused?

    a. Léon Blum
    b. Alfred Dreyfus
    c. Moses Hess
    d. André Maurois

**83.** Israel's first permanent delegate to the United Nations served from 1948 to 1959. His name is

    a. David Ben Gurion
    b. Chaim Weizmann
    c. Levi Eshkol
    d. Abba Eban

**84.** Chaim Herzog, one of the sons of the pre-state chief rabbi of the Ashkenazic community in Palestine was head of the Israeli army's intelligence division from 1948 to 1950. In 1983 he was selected as Israel's

    a. ambassador to the United States
    b. ambassador to the United Nations
    c. sixth president
    d. consul general in New York

**85.** During his first two years in office, President Bill Clinton appointed two Jewish justices to the Supreme Court. They are

    a. Brandeis and Cardozo
    b. Frankfurter and Fortas
    c. Goldberg and Ginsburg
    d. Ginsburg and Breyer

**86.** Founder of the Jewish Sunday school movement in the United States, this woman was the beautiful daughter of a wealthy Philadelphia philanthropist. Her name is

    a. Henrietta Szold
    b. Nelly Sachs
    c. Rebecca Gratz
    d. Emma Lazarus

**87.** This woman, who never married, was born in 1860 in Baltimore, where her father served as a rabbi for forty years. She was secretary of the Jewish Publication Society of America from 1892 to 1919. In 1912 she organized Hadassah, the Women's Zionist Organization of America. Her name is

    a. Golda Meir
    b. Henrietta Szold
    c. Frances Perkins
    d. Lillian Wald

**88.** After the 1992 elections, one U.S. state had two Jewish men serving in the Senate. That state is

    a. Wisconsin
    b. Florida
    c. New York
    d. Ohio

**89.** One of the most beautiful, intelligent, and courageous women in ancient Jewish history seduced army commander Holofernes and beheaded him. Her story is told in one of the fourteen books of the Apocrypha. Her name is

    a. Judith
    b. Tobit
    c. Deborah
    d. Miriam

**90.** When the Israelites left Egypt, under the leadership of Moses, the waters of the Red Sea (or Sea of Reeds) miraculously parted so that they could cross through safely. Who led the Israelites when a similar incident occurred at a later point in Jewish history?

    a. Elijah
    b. Aaron
    c. Joshua
    d. David

**91.** Uriah Phillip Levy (1792-1862) was an American naval officer. His great achievement was the

    a. appointment of Jewish naval chaplains
    b. release of Jewish sailors from duties on Yom Kippur
    c. abolition of corporal punishment in the U.S. Navy
    d. establishment of the first Jewish military chapel

**92.** It was once believed that five members of the crew of Christopher Columbus were Jewish. Recent research has proven that only one, Columbus's interpreter, was undoubtedly Jewish. His name is

    a. Solomon ibn Gabirol
    b. Luis de Torres
    c. Solomon ben Maimon
    d. Nachmanides

**93.** The first Orthodox Jew ever to be elected a U.S. Senator was Joseph J. Lieberman. In 1988 he ran (and won) on the Democratic ticket to represent the state of

    a. New York
    b. Illinois
    c. Indiana
    d. Connecticut

**94.** Born in Lithuania in 1865, this rabbi arrived in Palestine in 1904 and settled in Jaffa. In 1921 he was appointed chief rabbi of the Ashkenazic community of Palestine, a position he held until his death in 1935. Even secularists admired him because of his progressive attitude. His name is

    a. Avraham Yitzchak Kook
    b. Avraham Mapu
    c. Shlomo Goren
    d. Avraham Karlitz

**95.** Born in Austria in 1911, this man arrived in Palestine in 1934. For more than twenty-five years, since he was first elected in 1965, he served as mayor of Jerusalem. His name is

    a. Levi Eshkol
    b. Chaim Weizmann
    c. Ezer Weizman
    d. Teddy Kollek

**96.** Oliver Cromwell, Lord Protector of England (1653-1658), was sympathetic to the Jews, supporting the movement to readmit Jews to England. The prominent Dutch rabbi who influenced Cromwell was

    a. Solomon ibn Gabirol
    b. Yehuda Ha-Levi
    c. Manasseh ben Israel
    d. Baruch Spinoza

**97.** According to the Book of Genesis, Noah's ark came to rest on Mount Ararat. In 1825 an American writer proposed that a place of refuge be established for Jews on Grand Island (in the Niagara River, northwest of Buffalo, New York) and that the place be named Ararat. Who was he?

    a. Judah Touro
    b. Mordecai Manuel Noah
    c. Isaac Abravanel
    d. Noah Levy

**98.** In 66 C.E., at the outbreak of the Jewish rebellion against the Romans, who were then in control of Palestine, the Romans appointed this Jew to be military commander of Galilee. Nevertheless, he fought against the Roman legions while seeking accommodation with Rome. After his defeat, this man's life was spared and he was brought to Rome, where in 75 C.E. he wrote *The Jewish War* and in 93 C.E. *The Antiquities of the Jews*, a history of his people. His name is

  a. Philo
  b. Yochanan ben Zakkai
  c. Titus ben Vespasian
  d. Flavius Josephus

**99.** There have been seven presidents of the State of Israel since its inception in 1948. Chaim Weizmann was the first. The others included

  a. Abba Eban and David Ben-Gurion
  b. Amos Oz and Yitzhak Navon
  c. Chaim Herzog and Ezer Weizman
  d. Yitzhak Ben-Tzvi and Chaim Herzog

**100.** Shabbetai Tzevi (1626-1676), born in Smyrna, Turkey, gained a large following which believed him to be the Messiah. When Shabbetai predicted that the Sultan of Turkey would give up the throne and crown him king, the sultan threatened him with death. He was saved only when he

  a. agreed to leave the country
  b. paid the king a large ransom
  c. agreed to convert to Islam
  d. retracted all his predictions

**101.** Solomon Schechter was born in Rumania in 1850 and later studied in Vienna and Berlin. In 1890 he was named Lecturer in Talmud at Cambridge University, in England, and in 1901 was appointed president of the Jewish Theological Seminary of America. In 1896 and 1897 he spent a great deal of time working on the Geniza fragments discovered in

   a. Paris
   b. London
   c. Cairo
   d. Jerusalem

**102.** In 1992 two Jewish women of the same state were elected United States senators. They are

   a. Dianne Feinstein and Bella Abzug of Florida
   b. Dianne Feinstein and Barbara Boxer of California
   c. Dianne Feinstein and Barbara Boxer of New York
   d. Elizabeth Holtzman and Bella Abzug of New York

**103.** In 1973, after being refused permission to emigrate to Israel, the Russian computer scientist Anatol (Natan) Sharansky became a leader of the Jewish emigration movement. In 1978 he was sentenced to thirteen years of imprisonment. He, and others like him who were denied exit visas, were called

   a. refuseniks
   b. nudniks
   c. litvaks
   d. cossacks

**104.** Ethel Rosenberg, Julius Rosenberg, Jonathan Pollard, and Morton Sobel became household names during the twentieth century. They were all

    a. convicted as spies
    b. inventors of household gadgets
    c. discoverers of unusual criminal activity
    d. members of a presidential Cabinet

**105.** Titus, the mighty emperor who was the son of Vespasian, destroyed the Second Temple in the year 70 C.E. He was

    a. Roman
    b. Persian
    c. Babylonian
    d. Greek

**106.** The first Jewish woman to be appointed to the United States Supreme Court was

    a. Dianne Feinstein
    b. Barbara Boxer
    c. Bella Abzug
    d. Ruth Bader Ginsburg

**107.** Marie Syrkin wrote *Blessed Is the Match* based on a poem by a courageous young woman who parachuted into Yugoslavia in 1944 in order to rescue prisoners and organize Jewish resistance to the Nazis. The heroine's name is

    a. Anne Frank
    b. Hanna Szenes
    c. Mathilda Schechter
    d. Henrietta Szold

**108.** Thomás de Torquemada was a fifteenth-century Dominican who was appointed Grand Inquisitor of his country. He was largely responsible for the 1492 expulsion of the Jews from

    a. France
    b. Spain
    c. Italy
    d. Germany

**109.** Several years prior to the destruction of the Second Temple in Jerusalem in the year 70 C.E., the Roman emperor Vespasian permitted one rabbi to leave Jerusalem peacefully to establish an academy in Yavneh, located near present-day Tel Aviv. The name of that man is

    a. Akiba ben Yosef
    b. Tarfon
    c. Hillel the Elder
    d. Yochanan ben Zakkai

**110.** Born in 1867, this woman was a dedicated social worker. In 1893 she founded the Henry Street Settlement in New York and was its director until 1933. She also organized the first nonsectarian public health nursing system and the first public school nursing system. She died in 1940. Her name is

    a. Golda Meir
    b. Henrietta Szold
    c. Lillian D. Wald
    d. Rebekah Kohut

**111.** Chaim Weizmann was born in 1874 in Russia and died in Israel in 1952. In 1948 he was elected the first president of the State of Israel. Although much of his life was devoted to Zionism, by profession he was a

    a. physician
    b. lawyer
    c. chemist
    d. physicist

# The Jewish
# Community

# 6

1.  In the middle of the eighth century, under the leadership of Anan ben David of Babylonia, a new Jewish sect was organized. Its adherents were called

    a. Karaites
    b. Samaritans
    c. Judeans
    d. Galileans

2.  B'nai B'rith, a Jewish service organization founded in 1843, has lodges all over the world. The Hebrew words *b'nai b'rit(h)* mean

    a. children of Israel
    b. sons of the covenant
    c. members of the tribe
    d. sons of Israel

3.  The Israeli organization known as Magen David Adom is the equivalent of the international organization known as the

    a. Red Cross
    b. Blue Shield
    c. Blue Cross
    d. Red Crescent

4.  In 1917 this organization was founded to protect the rights of Jews. Its organizer and most famous president was the ardent Zionist leader Stephen S. Wise. What is its name?

    a. American Jewish Congress
    b. United Jewish Appeal
    c. American Jewish Committee
    d. Jewish Defense League

**5.** An organization was founded in 1906 "to prevent the infraction of civil and religious rights of Jews in any part of the world." Its past presidents have included Mayer Sulzberger, Louis Marshall, Cyrus Adler, and Joseph M. Proskauer. It publishes a magazine called *Commentary*. The name of the organization is

   a. American Jewish Congress
   b. United Jewish Appeal
   c. American Jewish Committee
   d. American Jewish Conference

**6.** A group of anti-Zionist rabbis formed an organization in 1942 because they opposed the resolution of the Central Conference of American Rabbis (Reform) supporting the establishment of a Jewish state in Palestine. That group was called

   a. Union of American Hebrew Congregations
   b. Rabbinical Assembly of America
   c. American Council for Judaism
   d. Jewish Alliance

**7.** Sura and Pumbedita were famous as

   a. seats of great academies of learning
   b. the first cities to print a Hebrew book
   c. traveling performers in the Middle Ages
   d. outstanding talmudic scholars

**8.** Bar-Ilan is a famous Israeli institution named after Rabbi Meir Berlin (who changed his name to Bar-Ilan). The purpose of the institution, which was founded in 1955, is to

   a. educate young people
   b. heal the sick
   c. find homes for orphans
   d. care for senior citizens

9.  In 1965 the Institute for Higher Education was established in Beersheba, in the Negev, the southern part of Israel. In 1973 its name was changed to Ben-Gurion University of the Negev in honor of

    a.  Israel's first ambassador to the United Nations
    b.  Israel's first president
    c.  Israel's first prime minister
    d.  Israel's first military general

10. A Zionist organization that was founded in London in 1920 has done much to help Jewish children settle in Palestine. It has branches in fifty-three countries but none in America. What is its name?

    a.  WIZO
    b.  World Jewish Congress
    c.  Hadassah
    d.  Emunah

11. The basic program of Zionism was adopted at the First Zionist Congress in 1897. It is known by the name of the city where it was promulgated. The program is called

    a.  the Basle Program
    b.  the Cincinnati Program
    c.  the Geneva Program
    d.  the Paris Platform

12. Founded in 1923 and supported by B'nai B'rith, this organization services college students on most major college campuses. It is named

    a.  Hillel Foundation
    b.  Histadrut Ivrit
    c.  Jewish Welfare Board
    d.  Chabad House

13. Bezalel is a famous school in Israel founded in 1906 by Boris Schatz, a Latvian-born artist who studied in Paris. The main purpose of the school is to teach

   a. geography and calligraphy
   b. oceanography and archaeology
   c. arts and crafts
   d. synagogue furniture design and construction

14. During the seventeenth and eighteenth centuries, wealthy Jews in many countries of Central and Eastern Europe served as financial advisors and agents to the ruling class. They were called *Hofjuden*, meaning

   a. Court Jews
   b. Privileged Jews
   c. Favorite Jews
   d. Financial Wizards

15. The Jewish Institute of Religion, organized in 1922 by Rabbi Stephen S. Wise, merged in 1948 with an older Reform seminary that was situated in Cincinnati, Ohio. The name of that seminary is

   a. Hebrew Union College
   b. Hebrew Theological Seminary
   c. Yeshiva College
   d. Jewish Theological Seminary

16. A women's Zionist organization that has over 300,000 members in chapters throughout the United States was founded in 1912 by Henrietta Szold. The name of the organization is

   a. ORT
   b. Haganah
   c. Hadassah
   d. Emunah

17. The insignia of Yale University contains two Hebrew words which, according to the Bible, were originally inscribed on the breastplate of the High Priest. These words are

    a. *matzo* and *maror*
    b. *urim* and *tumim*
    c. *shalom* and *beracha*
    d. *mazal tov*

18. One of the first Zionist pioneering movements was founded in Kharkov, Russia, in 1882. It had as its motto the initials of the Hebrew words in chapter 2, verse 5 of Isaiah: "O, House of Jacob, come ye, and let us go." What was the name of this organization?

    a. BILU
    b. YIVO
    c. HIAS
    d. ORT

19. Louis Dembitz Brandeis was the first Jew ever to be appointed to the United States Supreme Court. He was appointed by President

    a. Warren G. Harding
    b. John F. Kennedy
    c. Woodrow Wilson
    d. Harry S. Truman

20. Chabad (also spelled Habad) is another name for the organization that is associated with the followers of

    a. the Lubavitcher rebbe
    b. Reconstructionism
    c. Rabbi Soloveitchik
    d. Jabotinsky

21. A school of thought which contends that Judaism is not only a religion but also a civilization was initiated by Rabbi Mordecai M. Kaplan. It has had a profound effect on many Conservative and Reform Jews. It is called

    a. Reconstructionism
    b. Liberalism
    c. Neo-Orthodoxy
    d. Conservatism

22. A scholar and educator who was born in Poland in 1911 became the president of Yeshiva University in 1943, succeeding Bernard Revel. His name is

    a. Louis Finkelstein
    b. Samuel Belkin
    c. Pincus Churgin
    d. Norman Lamm

23. The flag of Israel has a Star of David in the center and a broad horizontal stripe above the star and another one below it. The flag can be described as having a

    a. white background with blue stripes
    b. blue background with white stripes
    c. white background with black stripes
    d. yellow background with blue stripes

24. A Chevra Kadisha is a society whose function it is to

    a. care for all the details of a wedding
    b. care for the details of a Pidyon Ha-ben
    c. care for the details of burial
    d. recite Kaddish for those in mourning

**25.** The United Jewish Appeal was organized in 1939 to coordinate the fundraising campaigns of three organizations: United Palestine Appeal, American Joint Distribution Committee, and

    a. Zionist Organization of America
    b. American Jewish Congress
    c. National Refugee Service
    d. Hebrew Immigrant Aid Society

**26.** The group sent by the British to Palestine in 1936 to study the political situation, and which finally recommended the partition of Palestine into two sovereign and independent states, was called the

    a. Peel Commission
    b. Balfour Commission
    c. United Nations Commission
    d. Royal Commission

**27.** For many years, one of these institutions has given assistance to individuals who have immigrated to America from all parts of the world. Which one is it, and what do the initials stand for?

    a. JTS
    b. HIAS
    c. UAHC
    d. WJC

**28.** In 1968, in Brooklyn, New York, a group consisting primarily of young Orthodox Jews was organized to protect local Jews from attacks by blacks and Puerto Ricans. The group, which became known as the Jewish Defense League (JDL), was led by

    a. Rabbi Meir Kahane
    b. Rabbi Lee Levinger
    c. Rabbi Moshe Cohen
    d. Rabbi Moshe Levinger

**29.** The United Synagogue of America is an organization
of synagogues closely related to the

    a. Jewish Theological Seminary
    b. Hebrew Union College
    c. Yeshiva University
    d. Mirer Yeshiva

**30.** A college was opened in Philadelphia in 1909 to teach
Bible and rabbinics. Shortly afterwards, a department
of Hebrew and cognate languages was added. Funds
for the establishment of the school were provided
under the will of a Philadelphia lawyer whose father
was Jewish and whose mother was Christian. The
benefactor's name is

    a. Abraham A. Neuman
    b. Moses Aaron Dropsie
    c. Mordecai Manuel Noah
    d. Mordecai M. Kaplan

**31.** Max Nordau was born in Budapest, Hungary, in 1849
and died in 1923. He practiced medicine and also pursued a career in journalism. However, he is best known
for his efforts on behalf of

    a. the Zionist movement
    b. medical research
    c. the workingman
    d. Ethiopian Jews

**32.** The Institute for Jewish Research, formerly known as
the Yiddish Scientific Institute, was founded in Vilna
in 1925 and had branches in thirty countries by 1939.
It is popularly known as

    a. YIVO
    b. WIZO
    c. HIAS
    d. JWB

**33.** In 1945 a Jewish archive was established in Jerusalem. It is run by the Israel Martyrs and Heroes Remembrance Authority, which is assigned the task of perpetuating the memory of the Six Million killed in the Holocaust. The archive consists of museums, halls of remembrance, and many displays and sculptures. Its popular name is

   a. Holocaust Museum
   b. Holocaust Memorabilia
   c. Shrine of the Six Million
   d. Yad Va-shem

**34.** In 1807, one of Europe's leading rulers decided to reconstitute the ancient Jewish Sanhedrin (Supreme Court) because of charges that Jews were engaged in usurious moneylending. The name of this prominent leader is

   a. King Philip
   b. King George
   c. Napoleon
   d. Louis XIV

**35.** The National Federation of Temple Sisterhoods and the National Association of Temple Educators are related to which of these organizations?

   a. United Synagogue of America
   b. Union of Orthodox Jewish Congregations
   c. Union of American Hebrew Congregations
   d. Jewish Education Association

**36.** The synagogue is known in Hebrew as *bet knesset* or *bet tefila*. It is also popularly known by the Yiddish name

   a. shuk
   b. shul
   c. shilo
   d. shtetl

**37.** A prominent Jewish leader, an ex-president of the World Jewish Congress and the World Zionist Organization, reversed his attitude towards Israel at age eighty-five (in 1980), becoming one of its most severe critics. His name is

    a. Nahum Goldmann
    b. Stephen S. Wise
    c. Louis D. Brandeis
    d. Felix Frankfurter

**38.** During the Second Temple period the Sadducees were an important Jewish sect which held the belief that the Bible is to be taken literally. The major group that opposed them was the

    a. Nazarenes
    b. Nazirites
    c. Pharisees
    d. Karaites

**39.** A Hebrew theater company established in Moscow in 1917 was later transferred to Israel. In 1958 it took the name Israel National Theatre. Its Hebrew name means "The Stage." It is popularly referred to as

    a. Hadoar
    b. Haboker
    c. Habimah
    d. Haaretz

**40.** A special school was established in Jerusalem in 1949 to offer intensive Hebrew courses for the benefit of new immigrants to Israel. This type of school is called

    a. yeshiva
    b. midrasha
    c. ulpan
    d. kollel

**41.** The term *bet din* is most closely related to which of the following?

    a. bet knesset
    b. Sanhedrin
    c. bet ha-midrash
    d. bet tefilla

**42.** A secret organization was established in Palestine to protect the Jewish population during the rule of the British. It was created in 1920 and discontinued in 1948 when Israel became a nation. The name of the group was

    a. Haganah
    b. Hadassah
    c. Habimah
    d. The Stern Gang

**43.** Menachem Begin was born in Poland in 1913. In 1942 he arrived in Palestine and became the commander of an underground organization of fighters that battled the British. The organization was called

    a. Irgun
    b. Kibbutz
    c. Neturei Karta
    d. Haganah

**44.** Three major Jewish seminaries have been on the American scene for more than seventy-five years. The Hebrew Union College, which was organized in 1875, merged with the Jewish Institute of Religion in 1950. The Jewish Theological Seminary was founded in 1886, and the Rabbi Isaac Elchanan Theological Seminary was organized in 1896. Which one of these is part of Yeshiva University?

    a. Hebrew Union College—Jewish Institute of Religion
    b. Jewish Theological Seminary
    c. Rabbi Isaac Elchanan Theological Seminary

**45.** Beginning in 1904, many Jewish homes kept blue metal boxes into which family members deposited coins periodically. The money collected was sent to the

    a. Jewish Defense League
    b. Jewish National Fund
    c. American Jewish Congress
    d. Jewish Agency

**46.** The pilgrims were among the first to land on American shores in the seventeenth century. The Bible also speaks of pilgrims. Who were they?

    a. the first Hebrews to enter Egypt after Joseph became assistant to the king
    b. the first group to enter Palestine under Joshua after the death of Moses
    c. those Jews who visited the Temple in Jerusalem on Passover, Pentecost, and Tabernacles
    d. those Jews who were exiled to Babylonia

**47.** In the early 1930s, this organization was responsible for the transfer of young persons to Israel and educating them there. It was founded by Recha Freyer in response to German anti-Semitism. It was called

   a. Youth Aliyah
   b. Kibbutzim
   c. Eretz Yisrael
   d. Histadrut

**48.** An ancient Jewish sect that lived in the area between Judea and the Galilee believed that the Bible consists of only the Five Books of Moses. They built their own Temple on Mount Gerizim, adjacent to Nablus, the biblical city of Shechem. They are known as

   a. Samaritans
   b. Sadducees
   c. Karaites
   d. Pharisees

**49.** A fraternal insurance society was created in 1900 by Jewish immigrant workers who had recently come to the United States and Canada. In 1933, it helped to create the Jewish Labor Committee. Its Yiddish name is Arbeiter Ring. What is its English name?

   a. American Jewish Committee
   b. Hebrew Immigrants Aid Society
   c. Workmen's Circle
   d. Jewish Workers Guild

**50.** In 1917, a military unit of Jewish volunteers from Palestine, the United States, and Canada was organized to fight alongside the British during World War I in order to free Palestine from Turkish rule. The group was known as the

    a. Jewish Defense League
    b. Haganah
    c. Jewish Legion
    d. Stern Gang

**51.** Keren Kayemet Le-Yisrael, meaning "Perpetual Fund for Israel," and better known as the Jewish National Fund, was established by the World Zionist Organization in 1901 at the Fifth Zionist Congress. The original and primary purpose of the fund was to

    a. buy the land of Palestine back from Arabs
    b. supply funds for Jews to come and settle in Palestine
    c. plant trees in Palestine
    d. establish an endowment fund for kibbutzim

**52.** Stephen S. Wise, Isaac Mayer Wise, Kaufmann Kohler, Sabato Morais, Bernard Revel, and Cyrus Adler had one thing in common. They were all

    a. rabbis
    b. presidents of theological seminaries
    c. presidents of the Zionist Organization of America
    d. born in Europe

**53.** During World War II, one of these Jewish organizations serviced the soldiers and sailors in the military service. Which one is it and what do the initials stand for?

    a. JNF
    b. UJA
    c. JWB
    d. WJC

**54.** The first chancellor of the Hebrew University in Jerusalem was, early in his career, a practicing Reform rabbi in New York City. He was born in 1877 and died in 1948. His name is

    a. Abba Hillel Silver
    b. Mordecai Manuel Noah
    c. Judah Leon Magnes
    d. Judah Touro

**55.** The Knesset, established in Israel in 1949, consists of members elected to a four-year term. Its duties parallel those of the

    a. United States Congress
    b. United States Supreme Court
    c. United States Court of Appeals
    d. British House of Commons

**56.** The name of the well-known Israeli organization called Mapai is made up of the initials of the Hebrew words *Mifleget Poale Eretz Yisrael,* which means

    a. Israel Mapmakers Organization
    b. Israel Manufacturers Organization
    c. Israel Workers Party
    d. Israel Booksellers Association

**57.** Two Temples were built in Jerusalem. The first, built by King Solomon, was destroyed in the year 586 B.C.E. by Nebuchadnezzer of Babylonia. The Second Temple was destroyed in the year

    a. 333 B.C.E. by the Persians
    b. 70 B.C.E. by the Greeks
    c. 70 C.E. by the Romans
    d. 132 C.E. by the Syrians

**58.** This rabbi, born in Bohemia in 1819, has been called "Father of Reform Judaism in the U.S." He was the first president of the Hebrew Union College, which was organized in 1875 in Cincinnati, Ohio. His name is

    a. Joseph B. Wise
    b. Stephen S. Wise
    c. Jonah B. Wise
    d. Isaac Mayer Wise

**59.** There have been many controversies in Jewish history between individuals and schools of thought. One example is the dispute that took place between the schools of Hillel and Shammai. Which of the following groups could not have been in direct, face-to-face conflict?

    a. Samaritans and Reconstructionists
    b. chassidim and mitnagdim
    c. Pharisees and Sadducees
    d. Karaites and Sadducees

**60.** Since its inception in 1901, Nobel Prizes were awarded to almost four hundred individuals. Of that number approximately how many winners were Jews?

    a. ten
    b. twenty
    c. sixty
    d. one hundred

**61.** The Nobel Prizes were established from a fund of about $9,000,000 left by Alfred Nobel, the Swedish millionaire and inventor of dynamite who died in 1896. Prizes were to be awarded in five fields of excellence: physics, chemistry, physiology, literature, and world peace. Quite a few Jews have won prizes through the years. In what fields did they excel the most?

    a. medicine, first; physics, second
    b. world peace, first; physics, second
    c. medicine, first; chemistry, second
    d. literature, first; world peace, second

**62.** The words *Crusade* and *Crusaders* carry a bad connotation for Jews because when the Crusaders began their trek toward Palestine,

    a. Jews were denied the right to join
    b. Jews became innocent victims
    c. Jews associated the words with the Cross
    d. Jews associated the words with Satan

**63.** In 1903 Joseph Chamberlain, Britain's colonial secretary, offered Theodor Herzl a portion of territory in one of their East African colonies where Jews could settle and establish a homeland. That plan was called the

    a. Uganda Scheme
    b. Ethiopian Plan
    c. Ararat Settlement
    d. Birobidzhan Plan

**64.** In the second half of the eighth century, a group of Jews led by Anan ben David declared that the laws instituted by the Rabbis of the Talmud were not binding upon them. The group was known as Karaites because they

    a. believed only in the laws of the Torah
    b. believed only in the teachings of the Prophets
    c. were followers of the teachings of Ezra and Nehemiah
    d. believed only in the Ten Commandments

**65.** Jews who lived in Ethiopia were brought to Israel in the 1980s in two major airlifts: Operation Moses and Operation Solomon. These Jews are known as

    a. Karaites
    b. Sadducees
    c. Falashas
    d. Pharisees

**66.** An order issued by General Ulysses S. Grant in December 1862 expelled all Jews from the entire Tennessee Department for profiteering. It was revoked by President Lincoln because

    a. it singled out Jewish businessmen unfairly
    b. it was not sanctioned by Congress
    c. Grant acted without authority
    d. all Jews voluntarily resigned from the department

**67.** In 1920, when Palestine was under British rule, a secret Jewish underground army was formed to protect Jewish settlements against Arab attacks. This army was called

    a. Havdala
    b. Hadassah
    c. Haggadah
    d. Haganah

**68.** In Spain and Portugal during the closing years of the fifteenth century, many Jews were forced to accept Christianity or lose their lives. Outwardly, they acted like Christians, but secretly, behind closed doors, they practiced Judaism. These Jews and their descendants were known as

    a. Pharisees
    b. Marranos
    c. Karaites
    d. Sadducees

**69.** On September 15, 1935, at Nuremberg, Germany, the German Reichstag excluded Jews from holding German citizenship, from engaging in any kind of social intercourse with non-Jews, from employing non-Jewish domestics, and from participating in a range of economic activities. One was classified as a Jew if one

    a. worked for a Jew
    b. had a Jewish partner
    c. borrowed money from a Jew
    d. had two Jewish grandparents

# Significant Sites and Momentous Events 7

1. Under the peace accord signed by Israelis and Palestinians on the White House lawn on September 13, 1993, it was agreed that the first territories to be returned to the control of the Palestinians would be

   a. Gaza and Jericho
   b. Nablus and Gaza
   c. Jerusalem and Jericho
   d. Jericho and Hebron

2. Majdanek, Terezin, and Treblinka are best remembered in Jewish history as

   a. centers of Jewish learning
   b. the native cities of three great prophets
   c. Nazi extermination camps
   d. centers of commerce and industry

3. The *auto de fe* was a procedure instituted in Spain during the Inquisition, towards the end of the fifteenth century. At a public ceremony, sentences were announced. This was followed by public burnings of "heretics" outside the city limits. What is the actual definition of the term *auto de fe*?

   a. save the king
   b. praise the church
   c. act of faith
   d. for the glory of god

4. In September 1941, on the outskirts of Kiev, the Ukrainian capital, tens of thousands of Soviet citizens, mostly Jews, were rounded up, murdered, and buried body upon body in a ravine. That site is known as

   a. Babi Yar
   b. Auschwitz
   c. Treblinka
   d. Nuremberg

**5.** During the first century C.E. (between the years 6 and 66), Roman emperors sent in governors to rule Judea. These governors were called

    a. Hasmoneans
    b. Procurators
    c. Amoraim
    d. Inquisitors

**6.** Two cities in ancient Israel played an important role in biblical history and represented its northern and southern geographical boundaries. Dan is the northern city. The southern city is

    a. Jerusalem
    b. Haifa
    c. Beersheba
    d. Eilat

**7.** In 1950 the Israeli Knesset passed the Law of Return. This ruling allows any Jew

    a. who leaves Israel to return at any time
    b. to settle in Israel and become a citizen
    c. to become a citizen even if he refuses to live in Israel
    d. who has immigrated to Israel to return to his homeland if he so chooses

**8.** When Ben-Gurion, Israel's first prime minister, resigned from governmental service in 1953, he settled in a remote part of Israel. The name of that site is

    a. S'deh Boker
    b. Beersheba
    c. Eilat
    d. Nazareth

9. Blood libels occurred often in Jewish history. They were allegations that Jews murdered Christian children in order to use their blood for

    a. baking matza for Passover
    b. making wine
    c. making borsht
    d. dabbing on doorposts

10. One of the reasons why Buchenwald, a town in Germany about five miles northwest of Weimar, became well known is because in 1937

    a. the Weimar Republic was established there
    b. a new synagogue was built there
    c. the Nazis established a concentration camp there
    d. Hitler made a famous speech there

11. In 1979, Egypt and Israel signed a peace treaty in Washington, D.C., that had been worked out at secret peace talks held between Menachem Begin, Anwar Sadat, and Jimmy Carter at

    a. the White House
    b. Camp David
    c. Fort Knox
    d. Fort Benning

12. The first concentration camp, named after the village in which it was located, was opened in Germany as far back as 1933. The name of the camp is

    a. Auschwitz
    b. Dachau
    c. Treblinka
    d. Bergen-Belsen

**13.** The Dead Sea, located on Israel's border with Jordan, is the lowest spot on earth. People cannot drown in it and fish cannot survive in it because

    a. its oxygen content is too low
    b. its salt content is very high
    c. it does not contain hydrogen
    d. it is very shallow

**14.** In 1987, after twenty years of Israeli occupation of the West Bank (Judea and Samaria) and Gaza, an unexpected rebellion of Palestinians erupted. The uprising is referred to as the

    a. Hegira
    b. Inquisition
    c. Intifada
    d. Auto de Fe

**15.** Each morning, for six days, the Israelite forces under Joshua marched around the impregnable walls of a city. On the seventh day, after marching around seven times and blowing on rams' horns, the walls came tumbling down. The name of that city is

    a. Gaza
    b. Hebron
    c. Jericho
    d. Damascus

**16.** In 1967, in caves near the city of Jericho, about seven miles from Jerusalem, an Arab shepherd found manuscripts that turned out to be portions of the Bible that were written about 2,000 years ago. What was found were known as the

    a. Apocrypha
    b. Pseudepigrapha
    c. Dead Sea Scrolls
    d. Tosefta

**17.** A German word meaning "Night of the Broken Glass" refers to the eve of November 9, 1938, when the Nazis perpetrated a pogrom marked by the breaking of the plate glass on Jewish storefronts in Berlin, Germany, and other cities. This memorable night is popularly known as

    a. Kristallnacht
    b. Yom Ha-shoah
    c. Tisha B'Av
    d. Babi Yar

**18.** Martin Luther, leader of the Protestant Reformation of the sixteenth century, objected to both the vices and the authoritarianism of the Catholic Church. As a result of Luther's revolution, tolerance toward the Jews of Germany

    a. decreased
    b. remained the same
    c. greatly increased
    d. moderately increased

**19.** In the year 73 C.E., after a long siege, a large number of Jewish rebels committed suicide on a mountaintop rather than be captured by the Roman army. The mountain under siege was

    a. Qumran
    b. Masada
    c. Moriah
    d. Gerizim

**20.** On May 3, 1882, the Russian government enacted legislation which prohibited Jews from acquiring property in all parts of Russia except certain towns in an area called the Pale of Settlement. These laws, which were legally revoked in March 1917, were called the

    a. May Laws
    b. Blue Laws
    c. Jew Laws
    d. Pale Laws

**21.** A system of limiting the number of Jews (and other minorities) into universities was implemented in pre-revolutionary Russia. This system was called

    a. affirmative action
    b. numerus clausus
    c. May Laws
    d. Nuremberg Laws

**22.** One of the most devastating attacks on an Israeli town occurred in May 1974 when three Palestinian terrorists infiltrated from Lebanon and took 120 schoolchildren hostage. Their demand for the release of imprisoned Palestinian terrorists was rejected. The name of that town is

    a. Merchavya
    b. Ma'ale Adumim
    c. Ma'alot
    d. Masada

**23.** In 586 B.C.E., after the destruction of the First Temple, the Jews living in Judah, the southern part of Palestine, were sent into exile. The country to which they were exiled was

    a. Egypt
    b. Babylonia
    c. Syria
    d. Jordan

**24.** After World War I, a number of Russian czarist refugees (who had lost power to Russian communists) began to spread rumors among Americans that Jews were responsible for the Bolshevik victory. They produced forged documents that were supposedly the minutes of the secret meetings of the

    a. Sanhedrin
    b. Elders of Zion
    c. Jewish Defense League
    d. Irgun

**25.** Jewish legend describes a river that flows all week long but rests completely on the Sabbath Day. The name of the river is

    a. Euphrates
    b. Sambatyon
    c. Tigris
    d. Nile

**26.** A tribunal consisting of judges from the United States, the Soviet Union, England, and France met in 1946 to try twenty-one of the most notorious Nazis accused of inhuman activity during World War II. This trial was held in

    a. Paris, France
    b. Washington, DC
    c. Nuremberg, Germany
    d. London, England

**27.** The Sinai Operation came to a close on March 1, 1957 when

    a. Professor Sukenik of the Hebrew University announced the discovery of the Dead Sea Scrolls

    b. all patients at the Hadassah Hospital were granted free medical treatment

    c. Israel announced its intention to withdraw its troops from the Gaza Strip

    d. the Israeli army captured East Jerusalem

**28.** The airlift that brought almost 50,000 Yemenite Jews to Israel between December 1948 and September 1950 was termed Operation

    a. El Al

    b. Magic Carpet

    c. King Solomon

    d. King David

**29.** The site of the original Hebrew University buildings and the Hadassah Hospital is on a mountain in northeastern Jerusalem, overlooking the Old City. The name of that mountain is

    a. Moriah

    b. Scopus

    c. Ararat

    d. Hor

30. On the walls of the Arch of Titus there are depictions of the Goddess of Victory crowning Titus and of the march of Jewish captives carrying the Temple vessels after the destruction of the Second Temple. The arch is located in

    a. Jerusalem
    b. Alexandria
    c. Rome
    d. Cairo

31. This town in Poland, thirty miles west of Cracow, was the site of the largest Nazi extermination camp during World War II. What is its name?

    a. Auschwitz
    b. Augsburg
    c. Barcelona
    d. Prague

32. Bethlehem is sacred to Christians as the birthplace of Jesus. To Jews, Bethlehem is significant because it is the birthplace of

    a. King David
    b. Ben Gurion
    c. Chaim Nachman Bialik
    d. Naomi

33. A Babylonian city situated on the Euphrates River was an important center of Jewish culture from the third to the eleventh centuries B.C.E. The first great academy of Jewish learning was established there by Judah ben Ezekiel, and many great talmudic scholars conducted classes and gave lectures there. The name of the city is

    a. Barcelona
    b. Pumbedita
    c. Provence
    d. Baghdad

**34.** In 1928, the Soviet government, at the suggestion of President Kalinin, allocated a portion of Eastern Siberia for the settlement of Jews. Yiddish was to be recognized as the official language. The name of that region is

    a. Slabodka
    b. Birobidzhan
    c. Minsk
    d. Bukhara

**35.** The land that is today called Israel was called by what name in the days of the Patriarchs?

    a. Canaan
    b. Ur
    c. Sinai
    d. Moab

**36.** The Ezra Synagogue was built in Cairo, Egypt, in 882. In 1896 a large depository of sacred objects was discovered there. The most important articles found were

    a. old books and manuscripts
    b. silver candlesticks
    c. gold wine goblets
    d. pieces of the original Ten Commandments tablets

**37.** The Dome of the Rock, located on the Temple Mount in the area above the Wailing (Western) Wall in Jerusalem, is also known as

    a. Mosque of Medina
    b. Mosque of Omar
    c. Mosque of Mohammed
    d. Har Gerizim

**38.** Because of its rolling mountain ranges, the northern portion of the Land of Israel is called

    a. Negev
    b. Yarden
    c. Shomron
    d. Galilee

**39.** In 1516, in the city of Venice, a special area to which Jews were confined was designated. The site was called a ghetto because it was situated near a

    a. garage
    b. monastery
    c. circus
    d. iron foundry

**40.** During which of these Arab-Israeli wars did Israel capture the Golan Heights?

    a. Yom Kippur War
    b. War of Independence
    c. Six-Day War
    d. Sinai Campaign

**41.** The Negev, meaning "south" in Hebrew, is the generally dry, sandy desert that occupies two-thirds of Israel's land mass. The principal cities of the Negev are

    a. Beersheba and Eilat
    b. Eilat and Acre
    c. Haifa and Tiberias
    d. Eilat and Haifa

**42.** The Middle Eastern state where Esther, the heroine of the Purim story, played an important role is known today as

    a. Iraq
    b. Iran
    c. Syria
    d. Lebanon

**43.** After Joseph died, a new king became ruler of Egypt. The Israelites were forced into labor gangs and were treated cruelly. Among the structures they built were two storage cities named

    a. Sodom and Gomorrah
    b. Pithom and Raamses
    c. Gad and Asher
    d. Jericho and Goshen

**44.** Judah Touro was born in the United States in 1775. He was a wealthy merchant who helped George Washington finance the American Revolution. A synagogue bearing his name still stands in his home town and has become a national landmark. In what city and state is this synagogue situated?

    a. New Orleans, Louisiana
    b. Newport, Rhode Island
    c. Alexandria, Virginia
    d. Newport News, Virginia

**45.** Treblinka, Poland, was the site of a facility that became known the world over during World War II as a

    a. U.S. military reservation
    b. Russian evacuation center
    c. Nazi extermination camp
    d. Nazi military training center

**46.** Rachel, wife of Jacob and mother of Joseph and Benjamin, died on a road between two present-day major cities in Israel. These cities are

    a. Nazareth and Haifa
    b. Tel Aviv and Jerusalem
    c. Jerusalem and Bethlehem
    d. Jaffa and Bethlehem

**47.** The Bible speaks of one prominent leader whose burial place is unknown. That leader is

    a. Aaron
    b. Moses
    c. Jeremiah
    d. Joseph

# The Literary Scene 8

1.  This daughter of a famous one-eyed Israeli army general authored the novel *New Face in the Mirror* and a biography, *Her Father, His Daughter*. Her name is

    a. Ruth Dayan
    b. Rachel Dayan
    c. Yael Dayan
    d. Esther Dayan

2.  S. Y. (Shmuel Yosef) Agnon was born in Galicia in 1888. One of his famous books is

    a. *The Mishneh Torah*
    b. *The Bridal Canopy*
    c. *Tale of Two Cities*
    d. *Fiddler on the Roof*

3.  The outstanding English scholar Israel Abrahams was born in 1858. In 1888, together with Claude Montefiore, he founded *The Jewish Quarterly Review*. From 1891 to 1902 he served on the faculty of Jews' College, and he later taught at Cambridge. Which of these well-known books did Abrahams write?

    a. *A Guide for the Perplexed*
    b. *The Apocrypha*
    c. *Jewish Life in the Middle Ages*
    d. *The Caine Mutiny*

4.  Born in the Bronx in 1928, this American novelist, short story writer, and essayist published *The Pagan Rabbi and Other Stories* in 1971. In 1983 she wrote *The Cannibal Galaxy* and in 1987 *The Messiah of Stockholm*, a novel dedicated to Philip Roth. Her name is

    a. Mimi Albert
    b. Edna Ferber
    c. Rona Jaffe
    d. Cynthia Ozick

**5.**   Of these four Jewish classics, one has been issued in more editions than the other three combined. That book is the

    a.  Mishna
    b.  Talmud
    c.  Haggadah
    d.  Bible

**6.**   This German-born poet was co-recipient of the Nobel Prize for Literature in 1966 along with Israel's novelist S. Y. Agnon. On the eve of World War II she escaped to Sweden, where she created impressive poetry inspired by the Nazi Holocaust. Her name is

    a.  Emma Lazarus
    b.  Glückel of Hameln
    c.  Katherine Graham
    d.  Nelly Sachs

**7.**   Asher Ginsberg was a famous essayist and philosopher. He was born in the Ukraine in 1856 and died in Palestine in 1927, after having settled there in 1922. Among his well-known books are *Al Parashat Derachim* (*At the Crossroads*) and *Al Shetei Ha-se'ipim* (*Wavering Between Two Opinions*). His pen name was

    a.  Rambam
    b.  Ahad Ha-am
    c.  Sholom Aleichem
    d.  Ramban

8. This Jewish author was born in Poland in 1880 and died in Israel in 1957. Among his works, which were written in Yiddish and translated into English, were *The Nazarene*, *The Apostle*, and *Mary*. The name of this individual, who was widely criticized in many Jewish circles, is

    a. Chaim Nachman Bialik
    b. Shaul Tchernichovsky
    c. Sholem Asch
    d. Sholom Aleichem

9. The author of the 1970 bestseller *Love Story* and *Oliver's Story* (1977) also wrote the screenplay for the Beatles' movie *Yellow Submarine*. He is the son of a former New York City Reform rabbi. His name is

    a. Jerome Salinger
    b. Erich Segal
    c. Leo Rosten
    d. Philip Roth

10. Novelist Saul Bellow was born in Canada in 1915 and has taught at various American universities. One of his popular novels is

    a. *Gone With the Wind*
    b. *The Caine Mutiny*
    c. *The Adventures of Augie March*
    d. *The Fixer*
    e. *So Big*

11. A Jewish historian who was professor of Jewish history, literature, and institutions at Columbia University since 1930 wrote the following important works: *A Social and Religious History of the Jews*, *Modern Nationalism and Religion*, and *The Jewish Community*. What is his name?

   a. Louis Finkelstein
   b. Salo W. Baron
   c. Harry Wolfson
   d. Bernard Malamud

12. Morris Raphael Cohen (1880-1947) was an outstanding teacher and philosopher. His books on the logic of the natural and social sciences include *Reason and Nature* and *Law and the Social Order*. From 1938 to 1942 he taught at the University of Chicago, but he is best known for his years of teaching at another school. The name of that school is

   a. Yeshiva University
   b. City College of New York
   c. New York University
   d. Yale University

13. A prominent second-century talmudic scholar who was the teacher of the famous scholar Rabbi Meir embraced heretical teachings and was excommunicated by the Jewish community. Rabbi Milton Steinberg wrote a novel about this man, which he entitled *As a Driven Leaf* (1939). The scholar's name is

   a. Yehoshua bin Nun
   b. Akiba ben Joseph
   c. Elisha ben Avuya
   d. Simeon ben Gamaliel

14. A Jewish author who in his younger years had been a member of the Communist Party and even won the Stalin Peace Prize (1953) later had a change of heart and expressed it in *The Naked and the Dead*. Among his other writings were *Citizen Tom Paine* and *My Glorious Brothers*. His name is

    a. Edmond Fleg
    b. Howard Fast
    c. Arthur Miller
    d. Saul Bellow

15. David Moses Cassuto was a rabbi and scholar who was born in 1883 in Florence, Italy, and died in 1951 in Jerusalem. He was a professor at the Hebrew University from 1939 until his death. He is best known for his writings in the field of

    a. mathematics
    b. history
    c. Bible
    d. psychology

16. *The Wisdom of Ben Sira* [*Sirach*] was written in Hebrew by a Jewish sage who lived in Jerusalem in the second century B.C.E. This book, also known as *Ecclesiasticus*, was translated into the Greek and is one of the books of the

    a. Torah
    b. Prophets
    c. Hagiographa
    d. Apocrypha

**17.** Eliezer Ben Yehudah was born in Lithuania in 1858. When he came to Palestine in 1881, he changed his name from Perelmann to Ben Yehudah. He is most famous for

    a. writing a comprehensive dictionary of ancient and modern Hebrew
    b. the part he played in the War of Liberation
    c. teaching young actors and singers
    d. his works of fiction

**18.** This French-born author (1928) served in the Maquis during World War II and studied at the Sorbonne after the war. He is best known for *The Last of the Just*, his famous work about Jewish martyrdom that is based on the talmudic statement that the world is kept in existence through the merits of thirty-six tzaddikim (righteous men) in each generation whose identity is not revealed. His name is

    a. Émile Zola
    b. Leon Uris
    c. Isaac Bashevis Singer
    d. André Schwarz-Bart

**19.** One of the greatest Jewish philosophers of all time was born in Cordova, Spain, in 1135. He died in 1204 and, according to tradition, was buried in Tiberias (Palestine), where his tomb attracts many visitors today. This philosopher's famous work, *A Guide for* [or *of*] *the Perplexed*, has influenced not only Jews but such non-Jewish scholars as Thomas Aquinas, John Spencer, and Gottfried Leibniz. His name is

    a. Moses Maimonides
    b. Moses Nachmanides
    c. Moses Mendelssohn
    d. Joseph Caro

**20.** Benjamin of Tudela lived in Spain in the twelfth century. He is best known for a book that was published posthumously in 1543. The subject matter of that work is

    a. his travels to 300 different places
    b. his ideas on astrology and astronomy
    c. his interpretation of the Bible and Talmud
    d. the story of the expulsion of the Jews from Spain

**21** *For the Sake of Heaven, I and Thou,* and *Tales of the Hasidim* are important published works of a prominent German philosopher by the name of

    a. the Lubavitcher Rebbe
    b. Gedalia Bublick
    c. Martin Buber
    d. Abraham Joshua Heschel

**22.** The poet Chaim Nachman Bialik was born in Russia in 1873 and moved to Israel in 1924. One of his most famous poems is about a yeshiva student. It is called

    a. *Ha-matmid*
    b. *Ir Ha-harega*
    c. *Megillat Ha-esh*
    d. *Yeshiva Bochur*

**23.** The *Mishneh Torah*, written by Moses Maimonides in the twelfth-century, is a

    a. commentary on the Torah
    b. commentary on the Mishnah
    c. commentary on the Talmud
    d. code of Jewish law

**24.** An Austrian author born in 1881 wrote the pacifist drama *Jeremiah* as well as several successful biographies, including *Marie Antoinette, Mary Queen of Scots*, and *Joseph Fouché*. He lived in England for a while and then sought refuge from the Nazis in Brazil, where he committed suicide. His autobiography, *The World of Yesterday*, was published after his death. His name is

    a. Alfred Dreyfus
    b. Leopold Zunz
    c. Stefan Zweig
    d. Israel Zinberg

**25.** Abraham Cahan, a Yiddish journalist and editor, was born in Lithuania in 1860 and came to America in 1882. He was the editor of the Yiddish newspaper *Forverts* (or *Forward*) for about fifty years. He wrote an English novel entitled

    a. *King of the Schnorrers*
    b. *The Jewish Caravan*
    c. *The Rise of David Levinsky*
    d. *Making Good Again*

**26.** *Forty Days of Musa Dagh* and *The Song of Bernadette* are outstanding novels written by this Jewish poet and playwright who was born in Prague in 1890. He died in the United States in 1945, having moved there in 1940 after spending five years in England. His name is

    a. Samuel Goldwyn
    b. Franz Werfel
    c. Sholem Asch
    d. Robert Nathan

27. Rabbi Shimon bar Yocha'i, who lived in Palestine in the second century, shortly after the destruction of the Second Temple in 70 C.E., was buried on Mount Meron, near Safed, Israel. He is reputed to be the author of the

    a. Midrash
    b. Zohar
    c. Talmud
    d. Mishna

28. A professor of Talmud at the Jewish Theological Seminary, this prolific Lithuanian-born scholar authored many scholarly books as well as the popular seven-volume *Legends of the Jews* and *Students, Scholars, and Saints*. His name is

    a. Heinrich Graetz
    b. Simon Dubnow
    c. Louis Ginzberg
    d. Louis Marshall

29. Part of the Israel Museum in Jerusalem is an unusually shaped building called Shrine of the Book. In this structure is housed the

    a. first Bible ever printed
    b. first edition of all Israeli publications
    c. Dead Sea Scrolls
    d. Jerusalem and Babylonian Talmuds

30. One of the first novels to accentuate the problem of anti-Semitism in the United States was written in 1947 by Laura Zametkin Hobson. It was titled

    a. *Gentleman's Agreement*
    b. *The Victim*
    c. *All My Sons*
    d. *The Gallery*

**31.** One of the tractates of the Talmud that is studied more than any other is called *Avot* or *Pirkay Avot* in Hebrew. Its English name is

  a. Ethics of the Fathers
  b. Sayings of the Fathers
  c. Chapters of the Fathers
  d. Book of Proverbs

**32.** In the January 1990 issue of *Life* magazine, one hundred of the most important Americans of the twentieth century are listed. Sixteen of them are Jews, and only one is a woman. That person is

  a. Ruth Bader Ginsberg
  b. Betty Friedan
  c. Edna Ferber
  d. Margaret Seligman

**33.** This scholar, born in Poland in 1876 and educated in Germany, was professor of biblical literature at the Jewish Theological Seminary, in New York. He translated Dubnow's *History of the Jews in Russia and Poland* into English. In 1920, while on a relief mission in behalf of the American Joint Distribution Committee, he was murdered by bandits in the Ukraine. His name is

  a. Israel Friedlaender
  b. Moses Hyamson
  c. Solomon Schechter
  d. Alexander Marx

**34.** Judah Loeb (Leon) Pinsker was an outstanding pioneer of the Zionist movement. In 1882 he published a now-famous pamphlet which proclaimed that Jews could save themselves from anti-Semitism by the establishment of a Jewish state. The name of the pamphlet is

    a. *Der Judenstadt*
    b. *Birobidjan*
    c. *Auto-Emancipation*
    d. *Ararat*

**35.** This Pulitzer Prize-winning American author, born in 1915, wrote many plays, including *A View From the Bridge* and *Death of a Salesman*. He was briefly married to Marilyn Monroe. What is his name?

    a. Norman Mailer
    b. Arthur Miller
    c. David Merrick
    d. Irving Stone

**36.** The first part of the Talmud is called the Mishna and the second part is called the

    a. Machzor
    b. Siddur
    c. Gemara
    d. Talmud

**37.** A physician by profession, this illustrious poet and author was born in Toledo, Spain, in 1075. His religious and philosophical views were expressed in his famous work *The Kuzari*. His name is

    a. Yehuda Ha-Levi
    b. Ibn Ezra
    c. Moses Maimonides
    d. Joseph Caro

**38.** This author, born in Israel in 1936, is one of that country's most renowned novelists and short story writers. His first novel, *The Lover*, was translated from Hebrew into English and was also made into a film. His other popular novels are *A Late Divorce* and *Mr. Mani*. His name is

    a. Emil Ludwig
    b. Stefan Zweig
    c. Frederic Raphael
    d. A. B. Yehoshua

**39.** Leon Uris, born in Baltimore, Maryland, in 1924, is an outstanding American novelist. He wrote *Battle Cry* (concerning World War II) and *Mila 18* (about the uprising in the Warsaw Ghetto). Uris is probably most famous for his novel depicting the struggle for the establishment of the State of Israel. That book is

    a. *Exodus*
    b. *The Source*
    c. *The Naked and the Dead*
    d. *The Young Lions*

**40.** Born in Hamburg, Germany, in 1645, this fabulous woman, who was widowed while still quite young, wrote one of the most memorable memoirs in Jewish literature. Written in Yiddish, the work was translated into English by Marvin Lowenthal. Her name is

    a. Gluckel of Hameln
    b. Henrietta Szold
    c. Lillian Wald
    d. Beruria

**41.** An author and editor who was widely known for his unusual newspaper *The Carolina Israelite*, which was published in Charlotte, North Carolina, was also famous for his books of humorous essays, including *Only in America, For 2¢ Plain*, and *Enjoy*. His name is

    a. Saul Bellow
    b. Harry Golden
    c. Norman Mailer
    d. Arthur Miller

**42.** This multitalented author and political analyst was a special assistant to President Richard Nixon from 1968 to 1973. He later became an important columnist for *The New York Times* and won a Pulitzer Prize for Commentary in 1978. His name is

    a. David S. Broder
    b. William Safire
    c. Arthur Krock
    d. Paul Greenberg

**43.** Many famous Jewish personalities have had the surname Gordon. Aharon David Gordon (1856-1922) was an outstanding Zionist philosopher. Judah Loeb Gordon (1830-1892), known as Yalag, was a great Hebrew poet. Who was Samuel Loeb Gordon?

    a. a Hebrew author and Bible commentator
    b. a Nobel Prize winner for his work in physics
    c. a convert to Judaism who served in the British Parliament
    d. a literary critic

**44.** This German-born historian and Bible scholar wrote his monumental *History of the Jews* in German in eleven volumes between 1853 and 1875. It was translated into English and published in six volumes in 1891 by the Jewish Publication Society of America. The historian's name is

    a. Heinrich Graetz
    b. Simon Dubnow
    c. Israel Efros
    d. Alexander Marx

**45.** The American-born (1923) Harvard-educated novelist and activist who achieved immediate fame upon publication of his 1948 novel, *The Naked and the Dead*, is

    a. Herman Wouk
    b. Aharon Meged
    c. Amos Oz
    d. Norman Mailer

**46.** This sole Holocaust survivor of a Hungarian Jewish family wrote his first book in Yiddish in 1956. It describes his experiences in the Auschwitz concentration camp. In 1960 it was translated into English under the title *Night*. In 1986 he was awarded the Nobel Prize for Peace. His name is

    a. Irwin Shaw
    b. Heinrich Heine
    c. Elie Wiesel
    d. Aharon Appelfeld

47. An American-born (1929) Conservative rabbi wrote many popular novels, including *The Chosen, My Name Is Asher Lev*, and *The Promise*. His name is

    a. Herman Wouk
    b. Chaim Potok
    c. Amos Oz
    d. Aharon Appelfeld

48. This man, born in Russia in 1887, came to the United States in 1903. He taught Jewish literature and philosophy at Harvard from 1915 to 1958 and was promoted to professor in 1925. Among his important works are *Philo* and *The Philosophy of Spinoza*. What is his name?

    a. Louis Ginzberg
    b. Harry Austryn Wolfson
    c. Abraham Joshua Heschel
    d. Louis D. Brandeis

49. The author of the popular novels *The Caine Mutiny* and *The Winds of War* is a Pulitzer Prize winner who also wrote *This Is My God*, a book about the Jewish religion. His name is

    a. Sol Yurick
    b. Herman Wouk
    c. Jerome Weidman
    d. Irwin Shaw

50. This Jewish philosopher/rabbi/theologian, who was appointed in 1945 to be professor of Jewish ethics and mysticism at the Jewish Theological Seminary, was the author of *Man Is Not Alone* and *God in Search of Man*. His name is

    a. Elie Wiesel
    b. Simon Wiesenthal
    c. Abraham Joshua Heschel
    d. Alexander Marx

**51.** Saul (Shaul) Tchernichovsky was born in the Crimea in 1875 and died in Palestine in 1943. He was a physician by profession but gained fame as a

   a. poet
   b. scientist
   c. dancer
   d. novelist

**52.** Irving Stone, an American born in 1903, wrote novels and biographical fiction. His famous work *Lust for Life*, which was made into a movie, is the story of

   a. Rembrandt
   b. Michelangelo
   c. Vincent Van Gogh
   d. Leonardo da Vinci

**53.** Among this Polish author's best-known works are *The Family Moskat* (1950), *In My Father's Court* (1966), *The Magician of Lublin* (1960), and *Gimpel the Fool and Other Stories* (1957). Almost all of his works were written in Yiddish. His name is

   a. Isaac Bashevis Singer
   b. I. J. Singer
   c. Herman Wouk
   d. Gershom Scholem

**54.** The author of *The Unknown Sanctuary* (1928), born a Catholic, was in later years attracted to Judaism. He lived a full Orthodox Jewish life but never converted to Judaism. His name is

   a. Émile Zola
   b. Benjamin Disraeli
   c. Israel Zangwill
   d. Aimé Pallière

**55.** Naphtali Herz Imber (1856-1909) was a Hebrew poet who lived in Galicia, Rumania, Turkey, and Palestine. His most famous poem is

    a. *Adon Olam*
    b. *Hatikvah*
    c. *Yigdal*
    d. *Hallel*

**56.** A leader of Israel's Peace Now movement, in 1992 this author was the recipient of the German Publishers' Peace Prize. His novels, written in Hebrew, have been translated into English, French, and German. His popular 1968 novel *Michael Sheli* (*My Michael*) was made into a film. His name is

    a. Aharon Appelfeld
    b. A. B. Yehoshua
    c. Aharon Meged
    d. Amos Oz

**57.** This Prague-born writer described himself best when he wrote: "I consist of literature, and am unable to be anything else." When he died of tuberculosis in a sanitarium on June 3, 1924, he instructed his close friend Max Brod to destroy all of his unpublished manuscripts. The writer's name is

    a. Isaac Leib Peretz
    b. Sabato Morais
    c. Franz Kafka
    d. Theodor Herzl

**58.** The American poet Emma Lazarus (1849-1887) wrote a poem entitled *The New Colossus*, which gained great fame because it was inscribed on the

   a. Washington Monument
   b. Liberty Bell
   c. Statue of Liberty
   d. Tomb of the Unknown Soldier

**59.** Which of these business leaders started a famous bookstore?

   a. August Brentano
   b. Richard Simon
   c. M. Lincoln Schuster
   d. Abner Doubleday

**60.** Soviet poet and novelist Boris Pasternak was an apostate Jew who was born in 1890 and died in 1960. In 1958, after the publication of one of his books, he was awarded the Nobel Prize for Literature but refused to accept it. The name of the book is

   a. *Crime and Punishment*
   b. *Dr. Zhivago*
   c. *The Naked and the Dead*
   d. *Odessa Tales*

**61.** A famous English author born in 1864 of poor Russian parents in London earned his fame while teaching at the Jews' Free School. Among his better known books are *Children of the Ghetto* and *The King of the Schnorrers*. His name is

   a. Judah Touro
   b. Benjamin Disraeli
   c. Israel Zangwill
   d. Israel Abrahams

**62.** Many famous authors used Jews as leading characters in their writings: Shylock in Shakespeare's *Merchant of Venice*, Barabas in Marlowe's *Jew of Malta*, Fagin in Dickens' *Oliver Twist*. Who was the leading character in Sir Walter Scott's *Ivanhoe*?

    a. Rachel
    b. Rebecca
    c. Riah
    d. Ruth

**63.** An American author and art critic who was born in 1874 and died in 1946 settled in Paris in 1903 and became the center of a celebrated literary and artistic circle. She wrote *The Autobiography of Alice B. Toklas*. Her name is

    a. Edna Ferber
    b. Elizabeth Stern
    c. Cynthia Ozick
    d. Gertrude Stein

**64.** Carl Bernstein, Art Buchwald, Dan Kurzman, and David Broder are all outstanding

    a. journalists
    b. comedians
    c. artists
    d. athletes

**65.** This outstanding American author, critic, and educator taught literature at the New York New School for Social Research and other colleges. Among his writings are *On Native Ground* (a study of modern American prose literature), *Walker in the City*, and *Starting Out in the Thirties*. His name is

    a. A. B. Yehoshua
    b. Herman Wouk
    c. Arthur Miller
    d. Alfred Kazin

66. German-born (1897) Gershom Scholem settled in Palestine in 1923 and became associated with the Hebrew University. He emerged as one of the greatest scholars in the field of Jewish

    a. mysticism and kabbala
    b. history and geography
    c. physics and chemistry
    d. psychology and psychiatry

67. Menachem Ribalow (1895-1953) was the editor of a weekly Hebrew magazine from 1922 (one year after his arrival in America from Russia) until his death in 1953. The name of the periodical is

    a. *Bitzaron*
    b. *Hatzofeh*
    c. *Hadoar*
    d. *Maccabean*

68. This German social philosopher was the son of Jewish parents who abandoned Judaism before his birth, in 1818. In 1848, together with Friedrich Engels, he wrote *The Communist Manifesto*, which ends with the slogan "Workers of the world unite!" He had only contempt for Jews and Judaism. His name is

    a. Alexander Marx
    b. Karl Heinrich Marx
    c. Groucho Marx
    d. Moses Mendelssohn

69. The musical *Fiddler on the Roof*, which opened on Broadway in 1964, is based on the writings of

    a. William Shakespeare
    b. Sholom Aleichem
    c. Leonard Bernstein
    d. Arthur Miller

**70.** Joseph ben Mattathias Ha-Kohen was a well-educated Palestinian Jew who in the year 66 urged Jews not to resist the Romans who controlled the land. This author of *The Jewish War*, *The Antiquities of the Jews*, and *Against Apion*, which are the major Jewish historical sources for this period, is better known by the name

    a. Nachmanides
    b. Maimonides
    c. Philo
    d. Flavius Josephus

**71.** An important Yiddish writer who was born in Russia in 1852 is still remembered for his stirring stories, many of which have been translated into English. Perhaps his most famous story is *Bontsche Schweig*, written in 1888. His first and middle names are Isaac Leib. His last name is

    a. Asch
    b. Singer
    c. Peretz
    d. Zweig

**72.** Born in New York City in 1928, she is the author of a number of novels, short stories, and critical essays. Among her works are the novel *Messiah of Stockholm* (1987) and three collections of short fiction, including *The Pagan Rabbi and Other Stories*. Her name is

    a. Cynthia Ozick
    b. Mollie Berg
    c. Gertrude Stein
    d. Bella Abzug

**73.** Shalom Jacob Abramowitsch is the given name of a famous Hebrew and Yiddish author who was born in Russia in 1836 and died in 1917. Among his famous books are *Fishke the Lame*, *The Meat Tax*, and the autobiographical novel *In Those Days*. His pen name is

    a. Sholom Aleichem
    b. I. L. Peretz
    c. Mendele Mocher Sephorim
    d. Der Nister

**74.** Ann Landers, the popular advice columnist, has a twin sister who is equally well known as a columnist. Her name is

    a. Grace Lichtenstein
    b. Abigail Van Buren
    c. Merryle S. Rukeyser
    d. Flora Lewis

**75.** A Yiddish author of Polish birth (1886) settled in the United States in 1907. He wrote hundreds of stories and novels, some of which were translated into English and other languages. Some of the better known of his works are *In Polish Fields*, describing chassidic life in the mid-nineteenth century, and *The Last Revolt*, dealing with the Bar Kochba period. The name of the author, who died in 1954, is

    a. Norman Mailer
    b. Joseph Opatoshu
    c. Sholem Asch
    d. Lion Feuchtwanger

**76.** In 1919 this Lithuanian-born author settled in Palestine. He was later appointed professor of modern Hebrew literature at Hebrew University. He wrote hundreds of essays on Jewish history and literature and two particularly important books on the life and times of Jesus: *Jesus of Nazareth* and *From Jesus to Paul.* His name is

    a. Joseph Klausner
    b. Judah Magnes
    c. Nahum Goldman
    d. Stefan Zweig

**77.** Lithuanian-born Abraham Mapu (1808-1867), a nineteenth-century literary figure, earned renown as the first person to

    a. discover a cure for rabies
    b. compose a Jewish national anthem
    c. write a Hebrew novel
    d. write a Yiddish novel

**78.** Sholom (Sholem) Aleichem (1859-1916) was called "the Mark Twain of Yiddish literature." He wrote poems, novels, and dramas in Yiddish, Hebrew, and Russian. Sholom Aleichem was a pen name. His real name is

    a. Zalman Shneour
    b. Sholom Spiegel
    c. Shalom Rabinovich
    d. I. L. Peretz

**79.** This American-born (1913) novelist and playwright drew attention to his talent when he wrote a one-act antiwar play entitled *Bury the Dead* (1936). But his novel *The Young Lions* (1948) brought him instant fame. The name of this author is

    a. Norman Mailer
    b. Justin Kaplan
    c. Leon Uris
    d. Irwin Shaw

**80.** Two well-known Israeli scholars and authors are siblings. Yeshayahu Leibowitz is a professor at the Hebrew University. His sister, Nechama, is a popular

    a. Bible teacher
    b. Talmud teacher
    c. poet
    d. novelist

**81.** A well-known author whose surname was Levin wrote *The Old Bunch*, *Compulsion*, *Eva*, and an autobiography, *In Search*. The full name of this author is

    a. Rachel Levin
    b. Shemaryahu Levin
    c. Meyer Levin
    d. Ira Levin

**82.** This author, born in 1915, became an Orthodox Jew after the death of his son. He wrote many best-selling novels, including *The Caine Mutiny*, *Marjorie Morningstar*, *Youngblood Hawke*, and the nonfiction *This Is My God*. His name is

    a. Norman Mailer
    b. Maurice Samuel
    c. Herman Wouk
    d. Meyer Levin

**83.** This woman wrote seventeen novels, more than 200 short stories, plus scores of film and radio scripts. Some of her bestsellers included *Backstreet* (1931) and *Imitation of Life* (1933). The name of this social-minded, liberal author is

    a. Fannie Hurst
    b. Erica Jong
    c. Lillian Helman
    d. Gertrude Berg

**84.** This Rumanian-born writer (1895) came to the United States in 1914 and authored such popular works as *Harvest in the Desert, The Great Hatred, The Gentlemen and the Jews,* and *Certain People of the Bible.* His name is

    a. Maurice Samuel
    b. Herman Wouk
    c. Theodore H. White
    d. Carl Sagan

**85.** In 1967 this author won the Pulitzer Prize for his novel *The Fixer.* It was based on the Beilis Affair, in which Menachem Mendel Beilis, a Russian Jew from Kiev, was falsely accused of ritual murder. His name is

    a. Bernard Malamud
    b. S. Y. Agnon
    c. Isaac Bashevis Singer
    d. Herman Wouk

# Arts, Entertainment and Sports **9**

1. After a brief career as a Major League pitcher, Al Shacht achieved fame as a

   a. radio broadcaster
   b. pantomime entertainer
   c. Major League coach
   d. Minor League manager

2. Many Schwartzes have achieved distinction. One in particular was an actor, producer and founder, in 1918, of New York's Yiddish Art Theater. He was born in 1888 and died in 1960. His first name is

   a. Maurice
   b. Adolf
   c. Rudolf
   d. David

3. Born in Tel Aviv in 1945, this sabra gave his first violin concert at age ten and was propelled to fame when he made a television appearance on *The Ed Sullivan Show*. His name is

   a. Itzhak Perlman
   b. Itzhak Stern
   c. Itzhak Shamir
   d. Yehudi Menuhin

4. The most famous Jewish Olympian of all times won seven gold medals at the 1972 Munich Olympics. His name is

   a. Hank Greenberg
   b. Harold Abrahams
   c. Gyorgy Brody
   d. Mark Spitz

**5.** Ilya Schor was born in Poland in 1904. He studied in Warsaw and Paris before settling in the United States in 1941. He is a well-known

    a. author and journalist
    b. artist and silversmith
    c. music conductor and composer
    d. sports figure

**6.** This motion picture producer and director of such great box office successes as *Jaws* (1975), *Raiders of the Lost Ark* (1981), and *E.T. The Extraterrestrial* (1982) produced and directed a widely-hailed movie in 1993 about a Polish non-Jew who saved over 1,100 Jews during the Holocaust. His name is

    a. Adoph Zukor
    b. Neil Simon
    c. Mike Nichols
    d. Steven Spielberg

**7.** Benny Leonard, Barney Ross, and Maxie Rosenbloom were all prominent

    a. playwrights
    b. poets
    c. professors
    d. pugilists

**8.** An All-American football star from Ohio State in 1932 and 1933 was characterized in 1955 by Coach Red Blake of Army as "one of the most brilliant thinkers in football." This player's name is

    a. Sid Gillman
    b. Marshall Goldberg
    c. Lucius Littauer
    d. Benny Friedman

9. One of the pioneers of modern boxing was founder and editor of the influential boxing magazine *Ring*. His name is

   a. Nathaniel "Nat" Fleischer
   b. Barney Ross
   c. Max Baer
   d. Howard Cosell

10. One of baseball's shining stars, this player was born in New York City in 1911. In the course of his long career he played for the Detroit Tigers and Pittsburgh Pirates. His career batting average was .313 in 1,394 games. His name is

    a. Henry (Hank) Greenberg
    b. Ed Kranepool
    c. Mickey Mantle
    d. Johnny Kling

11. The first Yiddish actress to gain recognition on the American stage was the heroine in Jacob Gordin's play *Kreutzer Sonata*. Her name is

    a. Molly Picon
    b. Bertha Kalich
    c. Vera Korene
    d. Fanny Brice

12. Fanny Brice was a Jewish comedienne who achieved her greatest fame for creating the character

    a. Little Orphan Annie
    b. Topsy
    c. Baby Snooks
    d. Mrs. McGoo

**13.** Edward Israel Iskowitz, born in 1892, was prominent in every phase of entertainment. He was president of the Jewish Theatrical Guild, the Screen Actors Guild, and the American Federation of Radio Artists. He is better known as

   a. Edward G. Robinson
   b. Eddie Cantor
   c. George A. Jessel
   d. Theodore Bikel

**14.** This entertainer was born in 1889 and died in 1966. A night-club and musical-comedy singer, she is known for popularizing the song "My Yiddishe Mamme." Her name is

   a. Fanny Brice
   b. Molly Picon
   c. Sophie Tucker
   d. Nora Bayes

**15.** Ernest Bloch was born in Switzerland in 1880 and moved to the United States in 1917. His major contribution was in the field of

   a. sculpture and painting
   b. science and medicine
   c. Jewish music
   d. architecture

**16.** Often called "the Yiddish Helen Hayes," this actress (1898-1992) was the first lady of the Yiddish stage for most of the twentieth century. She played in many comic roles with a Yiddish repertory company established by Jacob (Yankele) Kalish, whom she married in 1919. Her name is

   a. Roberta Peters
   b. Regina Resnik
   c. Elaine Malbin
   d. Molly Picon

**17.** Father and son basketball players had outstanding careers. The father, Dolph (Adolph), played for the Syracuse Nationals from 1949 to 1963. The son, Dan, played for the NBA Utah Jazz team and the Denver Nuggets. Their last name is

    a. Schayes
    b. Schechter
    c. Holman
    d. Auerbach

**18.** A Major League player from 1965 to 1972, Art Shamsky played for the Cincinnati Reds and the New York Mets. He reached the peak of his career in August 1966 when in four consecutive times at bat he

    a. hit home runs
    b. hit doubles
    c. hit triples
    d. was hit by the pitcher

**19.** One of the most famous collegiate quarterbacks of all time was Benny Friedman. When Grantland Rice picked his All-American team for *Collier's* magazine in 1925, he had difficulty choosing between Friedman and Red Grange of the University of Illinois. For what college team did Benny Friedman play from 1924 to 1926?

    a. New York University
    b. University of Michigan
    c. Columbia University
    d. Yale University

**20.** Sidney Franklin (1903-1976), whose original name was Frumkin, was the first Jew to take up the sport of

    a. mountain climbing
    b. cross-country skiing
    c. wrestling
    d. bullfighting

**21.** A relief pitcher in the Major Leagues for eleven years, this baseball player, although clubfooted, established a respectable 53-44 won/lost record and a 3.67 earned run average. Most of his career was spent with the Los Angeles Dodgers. His name is

    a. Hank Greenberg
    b. Lawrence Sherry
    c. Sandy Koufax
    d. Ron Blomberg

**22.** Dyan Cannon, Paulette Goddard, Lily Palmer, and Beverly Sills all assumed stage names. What was the given name of Beverly Sills?

    a. Samile Diane Friesen
    b. Marian Levee
    c. Maria Peiser
    d. Belle Silverman

**23.** Yosele Rosenblatt, Moshe Koussevitsky, and Richard Tucker had careers in common. All were

    a. cantors
    b. opera singers
    c. composers
    d. lyricists

**24.** Born Howard William Cohen in Brooklyn, New York, on March 25, 1918, this attorney became interested in sports after he was discharged from the U.S. Army in 1946. He became one of the most successful broadcasters of sporting events. He changed his last name to

    a. Cosell
    b. Barber
    c. Glickman
    d. Koufax

**25.** A Jewish sculptor born on the East Side of New York City in 1880 gained international fame for his busts of leading personalities, including Albert Einstein, Chaim Weizmann, Winston Churchill, and George Bernard Shaw. He settled in England in 1904 and was later knighted. His name is

    a. Jacob Epstein
    b. Marc Chagall
    c. Raphael Soyer
    d. Henry Dreyfuss

**26.** This Brooklyn-born baseball legend is one of the youngest players ever to be admitted to the Baseball Hall of Fame (1972). He signed with the Brooklyn Dodgers on December 14, 1954. In the course of his career he pitched four no-hit games and forty shutouts. His name is

    a. Johnny Padres
    b. Ed Kranepool
    c. Lefty Gomez
    d. Sandy Koufax

**27.** The Jewish entertainer whose original name was Berlinger hosted a popular television show from 1948 to 1953. Widely known as Mr. Television, his stage name is

    a. Irving Berlin
    b. Berele Chagi
    c. Milton Berle
    d. Joey Bishop

**28.** Born in England on January 15, 1899, he was one of the leading sprinters in British track history. His life story was the subject of a movie entitled *Chariots of Fire*. His name is

a. Mark Spitz
b. Isaac Berger
c. Charlie Chaplin
d. Harold Maurice Abrahams

**29.** This American composer, born in 1898, introduced jazz and the blues into symphonic music, as was effectively demonstrated in his *Rhapsody in Blue* and *An American in Paris*. His *Porgy and Bess* is one of America's favorite operas. The lyrics for much of his music were written by his brother, Ira. The name of the composer is

a. Frank Loesser
b. George Gershwin
c. Sol Hurok
d. Richard Rodgers

**30.** Called "rabbi" by his fellow players because he sported a beard for a while, this football star was an outstanding receiver for the Pittsburgh Steelers. In 1978, his best year as a pro, he caught 37 passes. His name is

a. Ron Mix
b. Sid Luckman
c. Randy Grossman
d. Marty Glickman

**31.** Acclaimed at one time as the world's best chess player, this man whose mother is Jewish claims to have never been a Jew. His name is

    a.  Bobby Fischer
    b.  Boris Spassky
    c.  Samuel Reshevsky
    d.  Lev Aronin

**32.** A well-known family of Yiddish actors began its career when its first member acted in Russia in 1878. They appeared in London in 1883. Members of the family included Luther, Sarah, and Stella. What is their family name?

    a.  Skulnick
    b.  Schwartz
    c.  Adler
    d.  Barrymore

**33.** One of the longest running Broadway plays deals with a love affair between a Jewish boy and Gentile girl. The play is called

    a.  *Funny Girl*
    b.  *Abie's Irish Rose*
    c.  *Hello Dolly!*
    d.  *Love Story*

**34.** A famous escape artist, the son of a rabbi, was born Erik Weisz in Budapest, Hungary, in 1874. He decided on a career as a magician and developed an act featuring escape tricks. His stage name was

    a.  Harry Weisman
    b.  Eric Weiss
    c.  Harry Houdini
    d.  Uri Geller

**35.** Born in 1918, this American musician became permanent conductor of the New York Philharmonic Orchestra. His compositions include *First Symphony: Jeremiah, Second Symphony: The Age of Anxiety*, as well as musical scores for such shows as *Wonderful Town, Candide*, and *West Side Story*. His name is

a. Leonard Bernstein
b. Arthur Rubinstein
c. André Previn
d. Fritz Reiner

**36.** In the Broadway play *A Majority of One*, the leading character falls in love with a Japanese financier but refuses to marry him because of their difference in religion. The actress who played this character died in 1966. Her name is

a. Gertrude Stein
b. Sophie Tucker
c. Gertrude Berg
d. Molly Picon

**37.** The first and only Jewish woman ever to win the Miss America crown was

a. Tina Louise
b. Michele Lee
c. Virginia Graham
d. Bess Myerson

**38.** Albert "Dolly" Stark was seen on many baseball diamonds during his years in the Major Leagues. What was his position?

a. National League umpire
b. Minor League coach
c. manager
d. first baseman

**39.** An American film producer who came to the U.S. from Hungary in 1888 founded the Paramount Picture Corporation in 1917. His name is

    a. Hal Prince
    b. Jack Benny
    c. Adolph Zukor
    d. Morey Amsterdam

**40.** One of Israel's most famous artists uses a unique style in which his designs change in appearance when viewed from different angles. His name is

    a. Marc Chagall
    b. Boris Schatz
    c. Yaakov Agam
    d. Jules Feiffer

**41.** A soloist and piano recording artist of great fame arrived in the United States from Poland in 1940. He is also well known for his piano compositions. His autobiography appeared in two volumes: *My Young Years* (1973) and *My Many Years* (1980). His name is

    a. Yehudi Menuhin
    b. Arthur Rubinstein
    c. Leonard Bernstein
    d. Moriz Rosenthal

**42.** The first Jewish players ever to make the U.S. Davis Cup tennis team did so in 1951. Their names are

    a. Mel Allen and Howard Cosell
    b. Louis Finkelstein and Samuel Belkin
    c. Dick Savitt and Herb Flam
    d. Joseph Fishback and Myron J. Franks

**43.** Yehudi Menuhin, born in 1916, is one of the world's greatest violinists. He made his debut at the age of eight and gained international renown very quickly. His younger sister, a gifted pianist, has a very unusual biblical name. Her name is

    a. Jezebel
    b. Hepzibah
    c. Kerenhappuch
    d. Elisheva

**44.** Only one Jewish player ever won a Major League batting crown. In 1935, while playing for the Washington Senators, he batted .349 to win the title. His name is

    a. Charles "Buddy" Myer
    b. Moe Berg
    c. Albert "Dolly" Stark
    d. Morris Berg

**45.** A well-known Jewish comedian whose original name was Benjamin Kubelsky later used the stage name

    a. Ben Blue
    b. Jack Benny
    c. Jackie Mason
    d. Jack Carter

**46.** Sometimes called the greatest professional basketball coach of all time, his team won the National Basketball Association title eight consecutive times between 1959 and 1966. Among the most prominent players on his team were Bob Cousy and Bill Russell. This coach's name is

    a. Mel Allen
    b. Arnold "Red" Auerbach
    c. Bernard "Red" Sarachek
    d. Abe Saperstein

**47.** Many entertainers have converted to Judaism. Which two of the following are Jewish converts?

    a. Dean Martin
    b. Louis "Satchmo" Armstrong
    c. Johnny Mathis
    d. Sammy Davis, Jr.

**48.** Marv Levy began his coaching career in 1969 with the Philadelphia Eagles. His career reached its high point in the 1990s when, as head coach of the Buffalo Bills, his team played in the Superbowl four times and

    a. won three times
    b. won twice
    c. won once
    d. never won

**49.** In 1914 a new comic strip character, Abie Kabibble, was created. He represented "the wandering Jew taking a short rest in the suburbs of the world." The creator was

    a. Albert Hirschfeld
    b. Harry Hershfield
    c. Max Fleischer
    d. Al Capp

**50.** The son of Russian immigrants, this actor's original name was Issur Danielovitch, which he later changed to Isadore Demsky. He played an American colonel in *Cast a Giant Shadow* (1966) and produced and starred in the Broadway play *One Flew Over the Cuckoo's Nest* (1963). His stage name is

    a. Danny Kaye
    b. Richard Dreyfus
    c. Kirk Douglas
    d. Paul Douglas

**51.** A well-known television and night club entertainer, the son of a cantor, made his Broadway debut in 1964 playing the lead in *What Makes Sammy Run?* He is married to Eydie Gormé, an equally popular singer. His name is

    a. Eddie Fisher
    b. Steve Lawrence
    c. Phil Silvers
    d. Jerry Lester

**52.** Jews have been chess enthusiasts for centuries. Rashi mentions chess in his eleventh-century writings, and it is believed that an eleventh-century scholar, Simeon the Great of Mayence, played a chess game with a pope. One of the great Jewish chess players, born in Poland in 1911, later settled in the United States. His name is

    a. Lev Aronin
    b. Max Blau
    c. Samuel Reshevsky
    d. Emanuel Lasker

**53.** Abe Saperstein, born in London, England, in 1901, has been called the "Barnum of Basketball." His famous all-Negro team is known as the

    a. Harlem Globetrotters
    b. Black Sox
    c. Knickerbockers
    d. Basketeers

**54.** This pugilist was world light-heavyweight boxing champion from 1930 to 1934. He gave up boxing in 1939 and became an entertainer. A famous nickname was attached to his name. He was called

 a. Rosy Rosenbloom
 b. King of the Ring
 c. Slapsie Maxie
 d. Maxie the Rosie

**55.** Richard Tucker was a successful synagogue cantor before he turned to opera. In 1945 he made his debut with the Metropolitan Opera in New York. Another Metropolitan soloist who also excelled in cantorial music was

 a. Rudolf Bing
 b. Jan Peerce
 c. Steve Lawrence
 d. Richard Tauber

**56.** Not too many Major Leaguers have hit four grand-slam home runs in their entire career. A Jewish star who played for the New York Giants in 1948 and for the Boston Braves in 1950 hit four home runs with the bases loaded in one *season*. His name is

 a. Ed Kranepool
 b. Sid Gordon
 c. Rod Carew
 d. Moe Berg

**57.** The famous Jewish composer who wrote "Promises, Promises" and "I'll Never Fall in Love Again" is

 a. Burt Bacharach
 b. Joel Grey
 c. Steve Lawrence
 d. Irving Berlin

**58.** This Russian-born (1888) son of a cantor composed the music and lyrics for many successful plays and movies, including *This Is the Army* and *Annie Get Your Gun*. He also wrote the popular song "God Bless America." His name is

    a. Irving Berlin
    b. Milton Berle
    c. Leonard Bernstein
    d. Sammy Cahn

**59.** The four Marx brothers—Leonard (Chico), Arthur (Harpo), Julius (Groucho), and Herbert (Zeppo)—were

    a. baseball players
    b. concert pianists
    c. comedians
    d. a choral group

**60.** In 1932, in Tel Aviv, more than 2,000 Jewish athletes gathered from twenty-two countries to participate in an all-Jewish sports spectacular conducted on the style of the Olympics. It was called

    a. Kaduree
    b. Jewish Olympics
    c. Maccabiad
    d. Machanayim

**61.** The Baltimore Orioles player named best pitcher in the American League for the 1980 season had also played for the San Francisco Giants, the Chicago White Sox, and the Chicago Cubs. His name is

    a. Ed Kranepool
    b. Don Drysdale
    c. Steve Stone
    d. Sandy Koufax

**62.** In what sport did Edward Gottlieb and Harry D. Henshel earn their reputations?

    a. football
    b. basketball
    c. baseball
    d. fencing

**63.** This Hungarian composer (1887-1951) settled in the United States in 1909. He wrote over two thousand songs and the operettas *Student Prince, Desert Song,* and *New Moon.* His name is

    a. Sigmund Romberg
    b. Oscar Hammerstein
    c. Oscar Straus
    d. Gustav Mahler

**64.** A famous American boxer who won the world heavyweight championship in 1934 wore boxing trunks with a Star of David on it, although he was not Jewish. He died in 1959. His name is

    a. Benny Leonard
    b. Max Baer
    c. Barney Ross
    d. Daniel Mendoza

**65.** A well-known entertainer who died in 1950 was the son of a cantor. His first musical sound picture was *The Jazz Singer,* in which he plays the part of a cantor. He is best remembered for his rendition of "Mammy," which he sang with his face blackened. His name is

    a. Eddie Cantor
    b. Al Jolson
    c. George Jessel
    d. Don Rickles

**66.** When John J. McGraw was manager of the old New York Giants baseball team, he searched the Minor Leagues for a "Jewish Babe Ruth." He was anxious to attract Jews to the Polo Grounds and thought he found the right man playing in El Paso, Texas. The player was

    a. Sandy Koufax
    b. Hank Greenberg
    c. Andy Cohen
    d. Dan Schayes

**67.** Cecil M. Hart (1883-1940), a Canadian, was a descendant of Aaron Hart, the first Jew to settle in Canada. Although completely absorbed in baseball in his early years, he is best known for his connection with another sport. The Hart Trophy is presented annually to the most valuable player in

    a. baseball
    b. basketball
    c. ice hockey
    d. soccer

**68.** An outstanding halfback, this star played for Columbia University from 1936 to 1938. In 1939 he joined the Chicago Bears professional football team as quarterback and was their leading player for many years. His name is

    a. "Battling" Levinsky
    b. Sam Jaffe
    c. Sid Luckman
    d. Terry Grossman

69. Abraham (Avraham) Soyer, an author and Hebrew pedagogue who taught at the Teacher's Institute of Yeshiva University until his death in 1940, was the father of Isaac and Raphael Soyer. Both sons were noted

    a. teachers
    b. doctors
    c. artists
    d. philosophers

70. One of the basketball "greats" of the twentieth century played professionally for the original Celtics and later became coach of the City College of New York, a position he held for almost forty years, up until 1960. During a 1949 visit to Israel, he helped establish basketball as a major sport. His name is

    a. Barney Ross
    b. Nat Holman
    c. Harry Henshel
    d. Red Auerbach

71. Jascha Heifetz was born in Vilna and settled in the United States in 1917. Before age five, he began making concert appearances and became one of the world's leading artists. The instrument at which he has shown his genius is the

    a. piano
    b. oboe
    c. violin
    d. viola

**72.** This young baseball player was voted Most Valuable Player and Rookie of the Year in the International League in 1965. In 1966 he won the Topps Award as the outstanding Minor League player, leading in home runs (29) and runs batted in (102). His name is

    a. Al Rosen
    b. Vic Raschi
    c. Mike Epstein
    d. Cal Abrams

**73.** A modern artist famous for his woodcuts on biblical and Jewish themes became a director of the New Bezalel School of Arts and Crafts in 1933. His name is

    a. Jacob (Jakob) Steinhardt
    b. Menahem Ussishkin
    c. Leon Uris
    d. William Steinitz

**74.** This artist, born in 1894 in the Polish city of Lodz, studied art in Paris and became famous for his book illuminations. He gained fame during World War II when he drew satirical anti-Nazi caricatures. He is well known for his illumination of the Passover Haggadah and both the U.S. and Israeli Declarations of Independence. His name is

    a. Marc Chagall
    b. Ben Shahn
    c. Arthur Szyk
    d. Yaacov Agam

**75.** Lipman E. Pike, the son of a Brooklyn haberdasher, was born in 1845 and died in 1893. In 1866 he played ball for a team called the Philadelphia Athletics and received $20.00 per week. He is considered to be the first professional

    a. football player
    b. basketball player
    c. baseball player
    d. soccer player

**76.** Lyova Rosenthal was born in New York City in 1931. She established herself as a first-rate actress in her portrayal of a neurotic young shoplifter in the Broadway drama *Detective Story* and as the "Jewish mother" in the film *Portnoy's Complaint* (1972). Her stage name is

    a. Lee Grant
    b. Fanny Brice
    c. Betty Grable
    d. Lillian Roth

**77.** Daniel Mendoza won a sports title in England in 1792. He was the first Jew anywhere in the world to win this title. The sport in which he was champion and about which he later wrote a rule book is

    a. tennis
    b. fencing
    c. boxing
    d. track

**78.** A famous boxer who held the world lightweight boxing championship (1934-35) and the world welterweight championship (1934-38) was

    a. Abe Goldstein
    b. Benny Leonard
    c. Barney Ross
    d. Jackie Berg

**79.** From 1901 to 1913 a Jewish catcher played with a number of clubs in the National League. He has been ranked as one of the great catchers of all time. His name is

    a. Al Rosen
    b. Johnny Kling
    c. Abe Simon
    d. Steve Stone

**80.** A New York attorney who began his association with basketball in 1967 saved the National Basketball Association from severe financial distress in the 1980s. His name is

    a. David Stern
    b. Arthur Goldberg
    c. Nat Holman
    d. Dan Schayes

**81.** This world-renowned actress was born in Paris in 1844 and educated as a Catholic. In 1915 one of her legs was amputated, but she continued with her acting career until her death in 1923. Her name is

    a. Eva Marie Saint
    b. Clara Bow
    c. Sarah Bernhardt
    d. Ada Reeve

**82.** A famous musician born in Germany in 1832 came to the United States with his family in 1871. His two sons, Walter and Frank, were (like their father, whose first name was Leopold) outstanding conductors and composers. The family name is

    a. Marx
    b. Damrosch
    c. Bernstein
    d. Adler

83. This actress was born Shirley Schrift, in St. Louis, Missouri, in 1923. She starred on stage in the musical *Minnie's Boys* (1970), in the comedy film *Over the Brooklyn Bridge* (1984), and in the dramatic film *Diary of Anne Frank* (1959). Her stage name is

    a. Shelley Winters
    b. Shirley Booth
    c. Sarah Vaughn
    d. Sara Mae Berman

84. The original name of the great comedian Ed Wynn, who won fame for his performance in *The Wizard of Oz*, was

    a. Isaiah Leopold
    b. Edward Lamm
    c. Eddie Horowitz
    d. Ed Newman

85. Kurt Baum, Mario Ancona, Jan Peerce, and Richard Tucker were all Metropolitan Opera stars. They shared the fact that they were

    a. baritones
    b. altos
    c. tenors
    d. bass-baritones

86. The stained-glass windows at the Hadassah Medical Center in Jerusalem are the work of the artist

    a. Ben Shahn
    b. Marc Chagall
    c. Saul Raskin
    d. Uri Shulevitz

**87.** Born in New York City on September 16, 1926, Bette Perske developed into a fine actress. She became famous after playing an important role opposite Humphrey Bogart in the 1944 film *To Have and Have Not*. She married her costar in 1945. Her stage name is

    a. Barbra Streisand
    b. Eydie Gormé
    c. Roberta Peter
    d. Lauren Bacall

**88.** In the early part of the twentieth century, the Jews of Vienna organized an intensive program of physical education in Jewish schools. Out of this program, the Hakoah Club developed. Members of the club competed the world over in the 1920s. The sport they were engaged in was

    a. soccer
    b. lacrosse
    c. basketball
    d. track and field

**89.** On July 30, 1992, at the Barcelona (Spain) Olympics, this athlete was the first Israeli ever to win an Olympic medal. The star's name is

    a. Mark Spitz
    b. Harold Abrahams
    c. Barbara Breit
    d. Yael Arad

**90.** Considered by many to be the greatest Jewish pugilist of all time, this boxer held the world lightweight title from 1917 to 1924. His name is

    a. Max Baer
    b. Battling Levinsky
    c. Daniel Mendoza
    d. Benny Leonard

**91.** Maria Peiser, Marian Levee, and Catherine Holzman changed their names before they became famous actors and actresses. The stage name of Marian Levee became

    a. Fanny Brice
    b. Simone Signoret
    c. Lee Grant
    d. Paulette Goddard

**92.** *Broken Glass*, a drama by a prominent American playwright, ran briefly on Broadway during the 1993-94 season. The play shows the effects of *Kristallnacht* on a Jewish couple. The author of *Broken Glass* is

    a. Neil Simon
    b. Arthur Miller
    c. Wendy Wasserstein
    d. David Mamet

**93.** The Israel Philharmonic Orchestra, founded in 1936 as the Palestine Symphony Orchestra, was conducted for many years by a non-Jewish musical director. His name is

    a. Yitzhak Perlman
    b. Isaac Stern
    c. Arthur Fiedler
    d. Zubin Mehta

# Answers

## Chapter 1
## The Bible

1. **(a)** The first five of the thirty-nine books are the Torah, the Five Books of Moses; the next twenty-one comprise the Prophets; and the last group of thirteen are the Holy Writings (Hagiographa).

2. **(a, b)** The snake spoke to Eve, and Balaam's donkey spoke out and complained to him.

3. **(c, d)** Moses did not appear before Pharaoh for forty days and forty nights. Joshua and a group of Israelites walked around the walls of Jericho for seven days, not forty.

4. **(a)** The Torah is called the Written Law and the Talmud is called the Oral Law. Originally, the teachings of the Talmud were passed on from generation to generation by word of mouth.

5. **(a, d)** The Book of Daniel and the Book of Ezra are part of the Hagiographa.

6. **(c)** Hagiographa is also referred to in Hebrew as *Kitvay Ha-kodesh*.

7. **(a)** Genesis ("Beginning") is the first book of the Bible.

**8.** **(b)** The Ten Commandments appears twice in the Bible: in Exodus 20 and, in a somewhat different form, in Deuteronomy 5.

**9.** **(a)** The story of the lives of the Patriarchs—Abraham, Isaac, and Jacob—is found in the Book of Genesis.

**10.** **(b)** Rashi lived several centuries before the other commentators.

**11.** **(d)** The Torah consists of only the first five books of the Bible. The Book of Jeremiah is part of the Prophets.

**12.** **(b)** Leviticus is part of the Pentateuch (or Torah), not of the Prophets.

**13.** **(a)** *Apocrypha* is a Greek word meaning "[books that were] hidden away."

**14.** **(a)** The Latin translation of the Bible is known as the Vulgate, meaning "common."

**15.** **(a, c, d)** Tobit, Judith, and Susanna are part of the Apocrypha. The others are part of the Bible.

**16.** **(c)** The Torah and Prophets are only part of the Bible, or Holy Scriptures. The Apocrypha is not part of the Bible.

**17. (e)**   Deuteronomy, from the Greek for "second telling," repeats many of the laws and events that are found in the first four books of the Bible.

**18. (b)**   Exodus tells the story of the Israelites in Egypt and their eventual release.

**19. (b)**   *Creatio ex nihilo*, meaning "created out of nothing," refers to the story of Creation in the Book of Genesis.

**20. (a)**   The fifth book of the Five Scrolls is the Book of Ruth. Judith, Tobit, and Susanna are part of the Apocrypha. The scrolls are called *Megillot* in Hebrew.

**21. (b, d)**   In later times God was referred to as Ha-Shem or Adoshem, which is a contraction of Adonai and Ha-Shem.

**22. (a)**   Man and woman were created on the sixth day, the last day of Creation. The seventh day was a day of rest.

**23. (b)**   The first sentence reads: "In the beginning God created heaven and earth."

**24. (c)**   See the Book of Genesis, chapter 2.

25. **(a, b, c)** The Bible does not identify the fruit eaten by Adam and Eve. Jonah was swallowed up by a "big fish," not necessarily a whale. Mordecai was Esther's cousin, not her uncle.

26. **(a)** Adam was so named because he was formed from the earth.

27. **(a)** See Genesis 1:27 and Genesis 2:22.

28. **(c)** Adam was warned not to eat from the Tree of Knowledge, for if he did, he would surely die.

29. **(b)** The serpent tempted Eve to eat of the fruit of the Tree of Knowledge, and Eve in turn tempted Adam. Because of this, the serpent lost its legs and had to crawl on its belly eternally.

30. **(d)** Samson fell in love with the Philistine woman Delilah but never married her.

31. **(c)** Aaron accompanied Moses when he appeared before Pharaoh.

32. **(c)** The Priests or Kohanim, as they are called in Hebrew are direct descendants of Aaron's family.

**33.** **(b)** Egyptian magicians were able to perform the same feat. See Exodus 7:8-13.

**34.** **(c)** In order to fulfill their request, Aaron asked the Israelites to give him their gold jewelry, which he then cast into a Golden Calf.

**35.** **(a)** Abigail was originally Nabal's wife. Nabal refused to provide David with provisions when he was fleeing from King Saul, who was determined to kill him.

**36.** **(a)** *Akeda* means "binding." This episode is recounted in chapter 22 of the Book of Genesis.

**37.** **(b)** See chapter 11 in the Book of Judges.

**38.** **(c)** See chapter 23 in the Book of Genesis.

**39.** **(a)** Joshua, Akiba, and Bezalel did not live during the period when Saul or David were kings of Israel.

**40.** **(d)** The traditional explanation for the omission of God's name is that since the Book of Esther was sent out as a letter to all communities, it might be treated irreverently.

**41.** **(a)** Hagar was also the handmaiden of Sarah.

**42. (b)**   Abraham's family continued to live in Ur, which is located in present-day Iraq.

**43. (a)**   Abraham was Rebecca's father-in-law. She was married to Isaac.

**44. (b)**   Hagar was Sarai's (Sarah's earlier name) Egyptian maidservant.

**45. (a, b)**   Neither Dinah nor Miriam was married to Abraham, Isaac, or Jacob. Rebecca was married to Isaac, and Leah was married to Jacob. Dinah was Jacob's daughter, and Miriam was the sister of Moses and Aaron.

**46. (d)**   Hillel is not mentioned in the Bible. He lived in the talmudic period, many centuries later.

**47. (d)**   Adam was the first man on the face of the earth.

**48. (c)**   The Amalekites blocked the way of the Israelites during their march through the desert towards the Promised Land. They slew the weak and weary stragglers. Finally, Joshua defeated the Amalekites in battle. See Exodus 7:8ff. and Deuteronomy 25:17ff.

**49. (c)**   Amos, the first of the literary prophets (775-750 B.C.E.), lived in Tekoa, about six miles south of Bethlehem.

**50. (c)**    The concept grew out of a mistranslation of Exodus 34:35, which reads: "The skin of Moses' face shone, sending forth beams [rays of light]." The Hebrew word for shine is *koran*, which is from the same root as *keren*, meaning "horn." Michelangelo's sculpture of Moses in the Church of Saint Peter in Chains (in Rome) depicts him with horns protruding from his forehead.

**51. (b)**    The structure they built was called the Tower of Babel.

**52. (c)**    Daniel's name was changed to the Babylonian Beltshazzar after he was appointed advisor to the king.

**53. (b)**    Daniel was thrown into a lion's den, but he was not harmed. Earlier, Daniel's three friends were thrown into a fiery furnace for refusing to worship an idol, but they also emerged unscathed.

**54. (a)**    Simeon and Levi, Dinah's full-brothers, agreed to allow Dinah to marry Shechem if he and all other members of his clan would become circumcised. They agreed, and then Simeon and Levi killed Shechem and his father.

**55. (b)**    Ephraim and Manasseh were the two sons of Joseph. There was no tribe named after Joseph.

**56. (b)** The name of the Torah portion in which the Holiness Code is found is called Kedoshim, a form of the word *kadosh*, meaning "holy."

**57. (b)** These animals are deemed to be of unequal strength. The weaker donkey would be overburdened by the ox.

**58. (c)** Zamenhof created the new language in 1887. Esperanto consisted of a limited amount of grammar and was expected to become a universal language to help increase international understanding. He also published an Esperanto handbook in Hebrew.

**59. (b)** Jubilee year is called *yovel* in Hebrew.

**60. (c)** Jacob and Esau were the twin sons of Isaac and Rebecca.

**61. (b)** Esau accused Jacob of "stealing" his birthright, although he had in fact sold it to Jacob for a bowl of lentil soup and some bread.

**62. (c)** Laban falsely accused Jacob of stealing his idols. It was Laban's daughter Rachel, Jacob's wife, who stole her father's idols.

**63. (a)** Only the Hebrew word *Bereshit* and the English word Genesis have the same meaning. Deuteronomy ("Second Telling") is close in meaning to Devarim ("Words"). The other three English and Hebrew titles bear no relationship to each other.

**64. (d)** Seventy scholars were engaged in the task. For this reason the translation was called Septuagint, from the Greek meaning "seventy."

**65. (b)** Jacob worked for Laban for fourteen years in order to marry Rachel. Laban had fooled Jacob. Originally, he was to work for Rachel for only seven years, which he did. But Laban insisted that Jacob marry Rachel's older sister, Leah, first. Jacob then had to work for seven more years before he was permitted to marry Rachel.

**66. (b)** Bilhah and Zilpah were the handmaids of Rachel and Leah who became Jacob's wives. Tzipporah is an alternate spelling of Zipporah.

**67. (a, c, d)** The Bible does not prohibit the taking of prisoners.

**68. (a)** Rachel was the mother of Benjamin and Joseph.

**69. (b)** Jacob gave Joseph a coat of many colors.

**70.** **(a)**    Jephthah had gone off to battle the Ammonites and returned safely from the military encounter. He kept his promise by sacrificing his daughter.

**71.** **(b)**    Jacob rolled the stone off the mouth of the well so that Rachel might fetch some water. See Genesis 29.

**72.** **(b)**    Both Ahab and his wife were notoriously evil people.

**73.** **(a)**    Benjamin was Joseph's favorite brother. Both were sons of Rachel. Joseph wanted Benjamin to be caught with the goblet so that he would be returned to Egypt and remain close to him.

**74.** **(c)**    Pharaoh dreamed about seven cows and seven ears of grain.

**75.** **(d)**    The Book of Obadiah, the shortest book, has only one chapter. The Book of Psalms is the longest, with 150 chapters.

**76.** **(b)**    The king sent her away and selected Esther to be his wife.

**77.** **(c)**    Potifar was also the king's chief steward.

**78. (b)**   The story is told in Genesis 41. Joseph was freed from prison and was appointed to be in charge of Pharaoh's court.

**79. (a)**   In the dream, seven lean cows swallowed up seven fat ones. The king also had a dream about seven ears of grain.

**80. (c)**   Only the Ten Commandments were kept in the ark. Some Rabbis believed that the ark also contained the pieces of the first tablets that were broken by Moses when he came down from Mount Sinai and saw the Golden Calf.

**81. (a)**   According to the triennial cycle it takes three years to read the entire Torah at the Sabbath service, compared to the more common practice of completing the reading in one year.

**82. (d)**   Taryag is spelled *tav resh yud gimmel*, which have numerical values respectively of 400, 200, 10, and 3, for a total of 613. *Aseret Ha-dibrot* is the Hebrew term for Ten Commandments.

**83. (c)**   See Genesis 32. Yisrael can be translated as either "prince of God" or "wrestle with God."

**84. (a)**   Joseph recognized his brothers first. They did not recognize him.

85. (b)    Pharaoh welcomed Joseph's family with open arms. See Genesis 46-47.

86. (a)    The sun, moon, and stars represented Joseph's father, mother, and brothers.

87. (c)    His hair got tangled in a branch and the mule on which he was riding kept moving. Absalom was left dangling in the air. See Second Samuel 18.

88. (c)    These were the three friends of Job, as described in the Book of Job.

89. (d)    The prophet was Jonah. The fish later spat him out onto dry land.

90. (c)    Joshua had succeeded Moses as the leader of the Israelites.

91. (c)    The Book of Leviticus describes the duties of the Priests and Levites, all of whom were members of the Tribe of Levi. Leviticus is called *Vayikra* in Hebrew.

92. (c)    Sulfurous fire rained down upon the cities. See chapter 19 of the Book of Genesis.

93. (c)    See Exodus 19.

**94. (d)**   See Exodus 1:5 and Numbers 11:16. The number seventy figures prominently in other biblical and postbiblical references.

**95. (c)**   Leah and Rachel were married to Jacob. Sarah was Abraham's wife and Rebecca was Isaac's wife.

**96. (b)**   Zelophehad was a member of the tribe of Manasseh. Zelophehad died in the desert, leaving five daughters and no sons. Until this time, daughters could not inherit their father's property. But the daughters demanded their father's share in the Promised Land. As a result of their demands, new legislation was proclaimed permitting a daughter to inherit (if there are no sons). If, however, the daughter marries someone who is not a member of her father's tribe, she does not inherit. See Numbers 27.

**97. (a)**   Zipporah, Jochebed, and Miriam were related to Moses. Zipporah was his wife. Jochebed was his mother. Miriam was his sister.

**98. (c)**   Pharaoh's court people were also present.

**99. (c)**   Miriam, the sister of Moses, did the actual hiding.

**100. (c)**   Aaron was Moses' brother. Jethro was his father-in-law. Amram was his father.

**101. (b)**　　Both Moses and Aaron were punished for disobeying God, although only Moses struck the rock.

**102. (b)**　　*Canticles* is a Latin word meaning "song" or "chant." Song of Songs is also called the Song of Solomon.

**103. (b)**　　See Exodus 3 for the complete story.

**104. (a)**　　Gershom and Eliezer were the two sons of Moses and Zipporah. Gershom was the elder.

**105. (c)**　　Numbers 18:24 details the tithe given to the Levites.

**106. (c)**　　Noah also lived to a ripe old age. He was 950 years old when he died.

**107. (c)**　　It is read at the end of the evening (Maariv) and morning (Shacharit) services.

**108. (a)**　　The Minor Prophets are much shorter than the other prophetic books.

**109. (a, b, d)**　　Abraham's original name was Abram. Sarah's was Sarai. Daniel's name was changed to Beltshazzar.

**110. (a)**     Whenever Haman's name is mentioned during the reading of the Megilla on Purim, it is greeted by loud noises.

**111. (c)**     When Naomi left Moab and went back to live in Bethlehem, her native town, she was escorted by Ruth.

**112. (c)**     Nathan compared the king to a rich man who robbed a poor neighbor.

**113. (b)**     The parents of Samson and Samuel made such vows, promising to raise their children as Nazirites.

**114. (a)**     The sources of the Hebrew passages found in the tefilin are of Exodus 13:1-16 and Deuteronomy 6:4-9 and 11:13-21.

**115. (a)**     Shem, Ham, and Japheth along with their wives and Noah's wife entered the ark.

**116. (b)**     See Genesis 9:8-17.

**117. (d)**     When Noah got drunk he uncovered himself. Ham's brothers, Shem and Japheth, covered their father but Ham did not.

**118. (c)**     The raven was sent out first but never returned. Later a dove was sent out, and it brought back an olive branch. This proved that the flood waters were subsiding.

**119. (d)**   The Book of Numbers is basically about the sojourn in the desert. The Hebrew name for Numbers is *Be-midbar*, meaning "in the desert."

**120. (a)**   In Hebrew he is called Eliyahu Ha-navi, "Elijah the Prophet." At the Seder, the door is opened for Elijah's anticipated arrival, since it is believed that he will be the forerunner of the Messiah.

**121. (c)**   According to some scholars, Pithom and Raamses were cities in which grain was stored; others describe them as garrison cities.

**122. (d)**   Akiba is the only one of the six listed who is not mentioned in the Bible. He lived in the postbiblical period, from 40 to 135 C.E., several centuries after the Bible was finalized.

**123. (b)**   The plague of the firstborn, during which the eldest son in every Egyptian household died, was the final plague.

**124. (a, b)**   Of these five, only caterpillars and bees were not among the ten plagues.

**125. (b)**   Ruth adopted Judaism after her husband, Mahlon, died. She returned to Bethlehem with Naomi and eventually married Boaz, a relative of Naomi.

**126. (b)**     Saul was David's father-in-law. David was married to Michal, Saul's daughter.

**127. (c)**     David was the son of Jesse. He killed his opponent (Goliath) with a slingshot.

**128. (c)**     These two cities were destroyed because of their wickedness.

## Chapter 2
## Biblical Quotables

**1.    (b)**    Here Esau forsakes all privileges that are his by virtue of the fact that he is the older brother. See Genesis 25:31.

**2.    (c)**    The words were spoken by the Philistine giant, Goliath, when David appeared to fight him. See I Samuel 17:43.

**3.    (d)**    Moses made the same declaration when he came down from Mount Sinai and saw the Golden Calf. See Exodus 32:26.

**4.    (c)**    Rebecca had dressed Jacob in the garments of Esau to deceive Isaac so that Isaac would confer his blessing upon Jacob, her favorite son. See Genesis 27:22.

**5.    (c)**    Joseph hadn't seen his brothers for many years and had no news of his family. See Genesis 43:7.

6.  (c)    God said this to Abram, whose name was later changed to Abraham. See Genesis 12:1.

7.  (c)    The brothers said this to one another when they saw Joseph approaching them. See Genesis 37:19.

8.  (b)    Pharaoh made this statement after Joseph had successfully interpreted his dreams. See Genesis 41:39-40.

9.  (c)    So spoke Job in lamenting his sad fate. See Job 3:3.

10. (a)    Beth El means "House of God." See Genesis 28:12.

11. (d)    These words of hope can be found in the Book of Psalms 126:5.

12. (c)    This was David's lament after learning of the death of his son Absalom. See Second Samuel 18, 19.

13. (d)    See the Book of Psalms 23:1. Psalm 23 is often recited at funerals.

14. (a)    See Ecclesiastes 11:1.

15. (b)    See Malachi 2:10.

16. (a)     Abraham was commanded to sacrifice Isaac, the son whom he loved. See Genesis 22:7.

17. (d)     The identical words appear in Isaiah 2:4 and Micah 4:3.

18. (a)     God said this to Adam after Adam was placed in the Garden of Eden. See Genesis 2:16-17.

19. (b)     God said this to Abraham at the starting point of a bargaining session over the number of righteous people that would have to be living in that city before God would spare it from annihilation. See Genesis 18:28.

20. (c)     See Ecclesiastes 1:2.

21. (a)     See the Book of Proverbs 6:6.

22. (c)     See Job 1:21. Job uttered these words when he lost his sons and daughters and all his possessions.

23. (a)     In this statement Samson reveals the source of his strength to Delilah. See Judges 13:5.

24. (d)     See Jeremiah 29:7, where Jeremiah speaks in the name of God to the exiled Jews living in Babylonia.

**25. (a)**    This plea for salvation appears in the Book of Psalms 22:2.

**26. (a)**    This was uttered by Moses to God when God instructed him to demand of Pharaoh that Pharaoh free the enslaved Israelites. See Exodus 4:10.

**27. (b)**    God said this to Moses when Moses approached the bush that was burning but was not being consumed. See Exodus 3:5.

**28. (a)**    Chapter 31 of the Book of Proverbs praises the woman of valor (in Hebrew, *ayshet cha'yil*).

**29. (c)**    Little David makes this statement of defiance to the giant Goliath in I Samuel 17:45.

**30. (a)**    Rebecca said this to Abraham's servant, who is not named. See Genesis 24:19.

**31. (a)**    The words "You shall proclaim liberty throughout the land for all its inhabitants" appear in Leviticus 25:10.

**32. (a)**    Reuben said this to his brothers when they planned to kill Joseph. He planned to return and save Joseph from the pit. See Genesis 37: 21-22.

**33. (c)**    The hairy man to whom Jacob was referring was Esau. Jacob feared that his father, Isaac, would discover that he, Jacob, was misrepresenting himself by appearing in the guise of his brother, Esau. See Genesis 27:11.

**34. (b)**    The brothers of Joseph had brought back to Jacob the good news about Joseph. See Genesis 45:28.

**35. (a)**    The story of the Tower of Babel is told in Genesis 11:4.

**36. (b)**    Cain answered, "Am I my brother's keeper?" See Genesis 4:9.

**37. (c)**    This statement was made towards the end of Jacob's life, when he gathered all his sons about him and predicted their future. See Genesis 49:3.

**38. (a)**    Esau said this when he returned from the field and saw Jacob cooking a stew. See Genesis 25:30.

**39. (c)**    This statement of Hillel (sometimes called Hillel the Elder) is quoted in the Talmud (Shabbat 31a). The Golden Rule itself is found in Leviticus 19:18.

**40. (a)**     These words were spoken by Balaam, who was sent by Balak, king of Moab, to curse Israel but could not bring himself to do so. Instead he blessed Israel. The words were later incorporated into the prayerbook in the prayer that begins with the words *ma tovu*. See Numbers 24:5.

**41. (c)**     This quotation is found in Psalm 90.

**42. (c)**     See Judges 15:16, in which the strength of Samson is portrayed.

**43. (a)**     This was Adam's punishment for listening to Eve, who persuaded him to eat of the forbidden fruit. See Genesis 3:19.

**44. (c)**     For this reason the mother of Moses hid him in the bulrushes. See Exodus 1:22.

**45. (c)**     Along with his family, Noah took pairs of each animal species into the ark. See Genesis 7:1.

**46. (b)**     In order to test Job, at the suggestion of Satan God took away all of Job's wealth as well as his sons and daughters. See Job 1:1.

**47. (b)**     Jacob said this to his sons when they brought him Joseph's bloody coat of many colors. See Genesis 37:20.

**48. (a)** An angel said this to Hagar, who bore a child for Abraham when Sarah was unable to conceive.

**49. (a)** The episode is known in Hebrew as the *Akeda*, meaning "the binding [of Isaac]." See Genesis 22.

**50. (b)** "Thou shalt love thy neighbor as thyself" is verse 18 of chapter 19.

**51. (d)** From Genesis 44:33. The boy referred to is Benjamin, who was arrested for "stealing" Joseph's royal goblet.

**52. (c)** This is one of the two dreams Joseph related to his brothers. From Genesis 37:9.

**53. (a)** This is not a commandment at all. The commandment pertaining to the Sabbath is a positive commandment. It begins with the words, "Remember the Sabbath day to keep it holy."

**54. (b)** These words are part of the Second Discourse of Moses. See Deuteronomy 8:3.

**55. (b)** See Isaiah 11:6.

**56. (b)**    Two prostitutes, both mothers of newborn babies, lived in the same house. One baby died and each claimed the living one as hers. See I Kings 3. Solomon made the statement so as to determine which of the two was the true mother.

**57. (a)**    See Ecclesiates 1:9. Solomon was also known as Kohelet, which is the Hebrew name for the Book of Ecclesiastes.

**58. (b)**    This advice of King Solomon is in the Book of Proverbs (6:6).

**59. (b)**    The quote is from the Book of Psalms (90:12).

**60. (a)**    The quote is from the Book of Psalms (133:1).

## Chapter 3
## Holidays, Customs, and Rituals

**1. (b)**    Bialik (1873-1934) was born in Russia and settled in Palestine in 1924. Today, an Oneg Shabbat is sometimes also held on Friday night.

**2. (a, d)**    The ring must be placed on the most prominent digit of the right hand, that is, the index finger. The ring must be unadorned with gems so as to eliminate the possibility of the bride's mistaking its value.

3.   (c)   The bitter herbs (*maror* in Hebrew) eaten at the Passover Seder symbolize the bitter life of the Israelites when they were slaves in Egypt.

4.   (d)   Visitors to gravesites place stones on monuments to indicate that the living have come to pay their respects to the deceased.

5.   (a)   Shavuot begins seven weeks after the first day of Passover. The Greek term for Shavuot is Pentecost, which means "the fiftieth [day]."

6.   (b)   Only when the Torah is read can the Bar Mitzva be awarded an aliya and recite the Torah blessings. It is these two acts that are the essence of the Bar Mitzvah ceremony.

7.   (a)   The tefilin boxes are held in place on the arm and forehead by leather straps.

8.   (a)   *Adloyada* is a term derived from a rabbinic saying which declares that one is to be so deliriously happy on Purim, to the point of inebriation, that he can *hardly tell the difference* (the literal meaning of the term) between the phrases "blessed is Mordecai" and "cursed is Haman."

9.   (c)   It is permissible by law to name a baby after anyone, living or dead. However, in some communities (among Ashkenazim in particular), it is customary to not name children after living people.

**10.** **(c)** At the Tashlich ceremony, crumbs of bread are thrown into the water as a symbolic act of casting off sins. The ceremony is observed on the afternoon of the first day of Rosh Hashana. If that day falls on a Sabbath, Tashlich is observed on the second day of Rosh Hashana.

**11.** **(a)** The Bedikat Chametz ceremony is performed by traditional Jews on the evening of the day before Passover. It is a symbolic expression of ridding the house of all leaven.

**12.** **(c, d)** Nothing is to be eaten on Tisha B'Av, which is a fast day. Although there is no prohibition against eating blintzes on Purim, traditionally blintzes are eaten on Shavuot. Hamantaschen are associated with Purim.

**13.** **(c)** As its name implies, the Shiva period lasts for seven days.

**14.** **(d)** Some people refer to se'uda shelishit as *shalashudis*, a distorted Yiddish form of the original Hebrew.

**15.** **(b)** It is read on Shavuot, the holiday on which the Jews accepted the Torah, (as did Ruth). The phrase *zeman matan Toratenu* ("the time of the giving of the Torah") is used in connection with Shavuot.

**16.** **(c)**    To form a lulav "bouquet," three myrtles and two willows are placed in a sleeve next to the palm branch. As the bouquet is held in the right hand and the citron (etrog) is held in the left hand, a blessing is recited over them.

**17.** **(b)**    The term *afikomon* is derived from the Greek word meaning "dessert."

**18.** **(c, d)**    Yom Kippur and Asara B'Tevet are observed as fast days. Asara B'Tevet commemorates the beginning of the siege of Jerusalem in 586 B.C.E.

**19.** **(a)**    In Hebrew they are known as *Shalosh Regalim,* literally meaning "Three Foot [Festivals]." On these holidays in ancient times, Jews from distant places journeyed (by foot) to the Temple in Jerusalem in order to offer sacrifices.

**20.** **(c)**    The Book of Lamentations (called Echa [Aycha] in Hebrew) is read on Tisha B'Av.

**21.** **(c)**    Chamisha Asar Bi-Shevat is also called Tu Bi-Shevat. Tu, spelled *tet vav* in Hebrew, has a numerical value of 15 (9 + 6).

**22.** **(d)**    *Blech* is a German word meaning "tin plate." Today, the covering which helps spread the heat is most often made of aluminum.

**23. (b)**   A kosher animal must chew its cud and have split hooves. Cows and sheep fall into this category; horses and pigs do not. Undomesticated kosher animals, such as deer, may be eaten if properly slaughtered.

**24. (a)**   More wine is drunk on Passover. The drinking of four cups of wine at the Seder is mandatory.

**25. (d)**   It is popularly believed that Yizkor is recited on the last day of Sukkot, but Shemini Atzeret is not the last day of Sukkot. It is an independent holiday. Sephardic synagogues do not hold a Yizkor service.

**26. (a, b, c)**   Rosh Hashana, Yom Kippur, and Sukkot all occur in the Hebrew month Tishri. Purim is celebrated during the month of Adar.

**27. (a)**   The Nazirites and the Rechabites refrained from drinking wine, as noted in Numbers 6:3 and Jeremiah 35:6.

**28. (c)**   On holidays that fall on weekdays, five aliyot are distributed. On Yom Kippur, six aliyot are allocated.

**29. (c)**   The literal meaning of the phrase *bikur cholim* is "visiting the sick."

**30. (a)** Rosh Hashana is the first day and Yom Kippur is the last. This ten-day period is also referred to as the Days of Awe.

**31. (b)** The Bible had already been finalized by 165 B.C.E., when the events of Chanuka take place.

**32. (b)** In the Jewish calendar, leap years occur seven times every nineteen years.

**33. (c)** Passover begins on the fifteenth day of Nissan, and Sukkot begins on the fifteenth day of Tishri.

**34. (a, b, c, d)** All of these are true. The Hebrew term for jubilee year is *yovel*.

**35. (c)** A fish need not be slaughtered like other animals, since the amount of blood in its system is minimal. But, to be kosher it must have both fins and scales.

**36. (a)** The explanation most commonly offered is that the breaking of the glass is an important reminder that all of life is not joy and that one need be cognizant of that fact even when celebrating a happy occasion. Many scholars, however, believe that a glass was originally shattered to scare off evil demons who are usually intent upon disturbing happy events.

**37. (c)** Tabernacles and Sukkot both mean "huts." Tabernacles is derived from the Latin *tabernaculum*, meaning "temporary shelter" or "hut."

**38.** **(a)** The Book of Esther (9:22) declares that the holiday is to be observed by "feasting and merrymaking, and as an occasion for sending gifts to one another and to the poor."

**39.** **(a)** The ketuba spells out the monetary and other obligations the bridegroom assumes upon entering the marriage.

**40.** **(c)** The Rabbis of the Talmud considered girls to be mature when they reach the age of twelve years and one day.

**41.** **(c)** The Brit (also pronounced Bris) is performed on the eighth day after the birth of a boy (even on the Sabbath and Yom Kippur), unless the baby is ill, in which case the ceremony is postponed.

**42.** **(b)** The eruv enables observant Jews to carry objects, wheel baby carriages, and perform other types of "work" on the Sabbath within the delineated area. These actions would otherwise be prohibited.

**43.** **(c)** *Duchan* is the Hebrew word for platform. The Priests stand in front of the ark (which is on a platform) when pronouncing the Priestly Benediction. The blessings are stated in the Book of Numbers (6:22-27). While pronouncing the blessing they cover their heads with their prayershawls.

**44. (a)**     Halacha is sometimes defined as "law." *The Code of Jewish Law* contains all of the basic Jewish laws.

**45. (c)**     The fourth letter is *shin*. The letters stand for the four Hebrew words *nes gadol haya sham*, meaning "a great miracle occurred there." Since the establishment of the State of Israel, the word *po* (which begins with the letter *pay*) was substituted for sham, changing the phrase to "a great miracle happened here [*po*]."

**46. (b)**     Many non-Orthodox synagogues count adult females as part of a minyan, but traditionally only adult males are counted.

**47. (b)**     The story of Haman and his plot to destroy the Jews is read from the Scroll of Esther, the Megilla, on Purim. Haman was hung on the gallows that he had prepared for Mordecai the Jew. Haman's sons were also put to death.

**48. (a)**     Just as Yom Kippur is regarded as the final day of the Season of Divine Judgment and is marked by worshippers beating their breasts, so is Hoshana Rabba, the last day of Sukkot and the long holiday season, regarded as a final opportunity to avert the evil decree.

**49. (b, c)**  In Temple times salt was always used in the sacrificial system. The egg represents the Passover holiday sacrifice. In the early centuries, dipping of a vegetable into salt water was common practice at all meals. Salt was known to be an antiseptic, and the dipping was originally performed for health reasons.

**50. (b)** Lag B'Omer is a spring holiday. It occurs on the thirty-third day after the second day of Passover, which is the equivalent of the eighteenth day of the Hebrew month of Iyyar. Lag B'Omer generally falls during the month of May.

**51. (a)** *Shaddai* is written on the backside of the mezuza parchment and is often visible through the aperture of the mezuza container.

**52. (a)** The sandwich is called the Hillel Sandwich.

**53. (c, d)** Yom Yerushala'yim (Jerusalem Day, which celebrates the reunification of Jerusalem in 1967) is celebrated on the twenty-eighth day of Iyyar. Yom Ha-atzma'ut (Israel Independence Day) is celebrated on the fifth of Iyyar.

**54. (a)** Weddings are prohibited during the three-week period concluding with the ninth day of the Hebrew month Av (Tisha B'Av). This is the time of year when in 586 B.C.E. and 70 C.E. Jerusalem was sacked and its Temples destroyed; hence, it is a period of semi-mourning.

**55. (a)** These are Polish-Yiddish words derived from the German. The kvaterin (godmother) takes the boy from the mother and hands him to the kvater (godfather), who hands the child to the sandek, the person designated to hold the boy while the mohel (circumcisor) performs the operation.

**56. (b, d)** An individual is a Jew if his or her mother is Jewish, either by birth or by virtue of having converted to Judaism, or if the individual himself or herself has converted to Judaism.

**57. (b)** The lulav, etrog, and sukka are all connected with the Sukkot holiday.

**58. (d)** Only on Yom Kippur and Tisha B'Av is a full twenty-four-hour fast demanded. On other fast days, the fast begins in the morning, at dawn, and ends in the evening, after dark.

**59. (a)** *Yahrzeit* is the Yiddish form of the German word *Jahrzeit*, meaning "anniversary."

**60. (c)** *Kapparot* is the plural form of *kappara*, meaning "atonement." The custom stems from an early belief that it is possible to transfer pain, guilt, and sin to another object. Today, charity is given instead.

**61. (a)** The Kiddush also commemorates the Exodus from Egypt.

**62. (c)** After the keria ("tearing") is performed, mourners pronounce the blessing, "Praised art Thou, O Lord our God, who is a righteous Judge."

**63. (a)** Rosh Hashana is the only holiday that occurs on the first day of the month, except for Rosh Chodesh (the New Moon).

64. **(a)** Kosher animals can be eaten only if properly slaughtered, salted, and rinsed before cooking so that the maximum amount of blood is removed. Liver can be made kosher only by broiling, since it contains an unusual amount of blood.

65. **(b)** "Chad Gadya" is the last song sung at the Passover Seder.

66. **(b)** The Yaaleh Ve-yavo prayer is recited on Rosh Chodesh (New Moon) and pilgrimage festivals. In the Spanish and Yemenite rituals it is also recited during the Amida of the Musaf service of Rosh Hashanah and Yom Kippur.

67. **(b)** Kol Nidre is recited only at the evening service that ushers in Yom Kippur.

68. **(c)** Al Chet ("For the Sins") is a popular Yom Kippur penitential prayer.

69. **(a)** The intended sacrifice is known as the Akeda.

70. **(a)** Bokser, the chewy dried fruit of the carob tree, is also known as St. John's bread.

71. **(c)** Hadasim (myrtle branches) and aravot (willow branches) are used with the lulav (palm branch). S'chach is the covering of leaves or branches placed on the roof of the sukka. The pitom is the pointed protuberance at the tip of the etrog.

**72. (b)** The name of the selection is the popular Chad Gadya ("One Only Kid").

**73. (d)** Herring has long been a traditional Jewish food. Being inexpensive, it was commonly eaten by Eastern European Jews.

**74. (c)** In addition to a grogger other methods of producing noise are used, including blowing horns and stomping feet.

**75. (d)** Literally, the words *kinyan sudar* mean "acquisition by handkerchief." The ceremony is commonly practiced by Orthodox and occasionally by Conservative rabbis.

**76. (c)** It is sung by family members each night of Chanuka after the candles have been kindled.

**77. (a)** These fundamental laws, named after the righteous Noah, prohibit idolatry, blasphemy, murder, adultery, robbery, the eating of a limb of a living animal, and include one positive commandment: the establishment of courts of justice.

**78. (c)** The *prosbul*, from the Greek meaning "court," was a document declaring to the court that debts made prior to the sabbatical year shall be collectible, thus ensuring that the lender would not lose his money. *Shemita* is Hebrew for sabbatical year.

## Chapter 4
## The Language of Judaism

1. **(b)** Both *chag* and *yom tov* are terms for holiday. However, the literal meaning of yom tov is "good day."

2. **(c)** *Ibn* and *bar*, like *ben*, mean "son" or "son of."

3. **(a)** An *akshan* is a stubborn person, one not easily persuaded to accept a different viewpoint.

4. **(c)** These three prayers are recited several times during the Yom Kippur services.

5. **(b)** Literally, *tzedaka* means "righteousness," or "justice."

6. **(c, d)** They are called both *neginot* and *te'amim*. They are also known by the Yiddish word *trop*.

7. **(c)** *Talit katan* literally means "small talit." Sometimes it is referred to as *tzitzit* (plural, *tzitziot*), meaning "fringes."

8. **(b)** Adoshem is a word formed from Adonai and Ha-Shem, both being Hebrew names for God.

**9.  (b)**  *Tanach*, the Hebrew acronym for Bible, stands for *Torah*, *Neviim* (Prophets), and *Ketuvim* (Holy Writings), the three divisions of the Bible.

**10.  (c)**  *Aguna* means "chained woman."

**11.  (d)**  B.H., an abbreviated form of *b'ezrat Ha-Shem* is sometimes written or printed at the top of a communication.

**12.  (b)**  Adon Olam is often sung at the conclusion of a Sabbath service.

**13.  (a)**  The Hebrew word *aliya* also refers to the act of leaving the Diaspora and "going up" to settle in Israel.

**14.  (c)**  Sheva Berachot are recited in the presence of the bride and groom as concluding prayers to the regular Grace After Meals.

**15.  (a, b)**  Bavli and Yerushalmi are the Hebrew names, respectively, of the Babylonian and Jerusalem Talmud collections. The Jerusalem Talmud is also called the Palestinian Talmud.

**16.  (a)**  *Yad* means "hand" in Hebrew. The Torah *yad* is shaped like a hand with its index finger extended.

**17. (a)** *Yichus* is a Hebrew word meaning "distinction" or "pedigree."

**18. (b)** Israel's main currency note is the shekel. One hundred agorot make up a shekel. The *peruta* series was in circulation between 1949 and 1960.

**19. (c)** The Haggadah is the Passover Seder prayerbook; the Machzor is used on holidays; and the Siddur is used on Sabbaths and weekdays. The most popular Machzor is the one used on Rosh Hashana and Yom Kippur.

**20. (a)** Sorrel, or sour grass, is the chief ingredient of the traditional Jewish soup dish known as s'chav.

**21. (b)** A native Israeli is called a Sabra because of his tough-tender nature.

**22. (b)** *Balabusta* is a Yiddish word derived from the Hebrew *baalat ha-ba'yit*, meaning "mistress of the house."

**23. (c)** A Machzor is a holiday prayerbook. A piyyut is a prayer-poem. (Piyyutim are found in the Machzorim used on various holidays.) Amida, a Hebrew word meaning "standing," refers to the Shemoneh Esray prayer, which is recited while standing.

**24. (b)**   Ladino is based on medieval Castilian but is written in Hebrew characters.

**25. (a)**   The word *tagin*, meaning "crowns," is Aramaic. *Taga* is the singular form.

**26. (c)**   Every seventh year in the Jewish calendar is a shemita (shmita) year, during which land is allowed to lie fallow.

**27. (c)**   The Hebrew alphabet has twenty-two actual letters. The letters *kaf*, *mem*, *nun*, *pay*, and *tzadi* are written differently when they appear at the end of a word.

**28. (b)**   The actual meaning of *am ha-aretz*, as used in everyday talk, is ignoramus. Originally, the term referred to unlearned people who worked the land.

**29. (b)**   These prayer services are held every day of the week throughout the year. Shacharit are the morning prayers; Mincha the afternoon prayers; and Maariv the evening prayers.

**30. (b)**   A Jewish skeptic or atheist is called an *apikores*, a word derived from the name of the Greek philosopher Epicurus.

**31. (d)**   Genesis 6:3 also mentions this figure as an extraordinary lifespan.

**32. (b)**    Av is the fifth month of the Hebrew calendar counting from Nissan.

**33. (a)**    *Mitzva* literally means "commandment" and in the vernacular means "righteous deed." *Avera* literally means "sin" or "transgression."

**34. (b)**    Literally, *baal koray* means "master of the [Torah] reading."

**35. (a, b, c, d)**    All are correct. Cantor is a word derived from the Latin; the others are of Hebrew origin.

**36. (c, d)**    Lag B'Omer is a minor holiday in the Jewish calendar. *Le-hitra'ot* means "until we meet again."

**37. (b)**    All three are terms for cemetery. *Bet ha-kevarot* literally means "house of graves," while the others are euphemistic expressions. *Bet olam* means "house of eternity" and *bet ha-cha'yim* means "house of life."

**38. (a)**    A *badchan* is an entertainer who usually pokes fun at people and tells jokes.

**39. (b)**    All Hebrew blessings begin with the words *Baruch ata Adonai* ("Blessed art Thou, O Lord"). *Beracha* means "blessing."

**40. (b)**    In Yiddish and in Hebrew, an idler is referred to as a *batlan*.

**41. (a)**    *Havdala* means "separation [of the holy Sabbath Day from the other days of the week]."

**42. (a)**    The Bedikat Chametz ceremony, conducted on the night before the Seder, involves the search for unleavened bread. The Biur Chametz ceremony, conducted on the morning of the Seder, involves the burning up of the unleavened bread.

**43. (c)**    The *ner tamid*, meaning "perpetual lamp," is first mentioned in Leviticus 6:6.

**44. (b)**    These are the names of popular prayers found in the prayerbook.

**45. (c)**    Literally, the Hebrew word *nachas* means "rest, restfulness."

**46. (c)**    This term, meaning "happy holiday," is the equivalent of the Yiddish expression a *guten yontif.*

**47. (d)**    *Chai* is spelled chet, which has a value of 8, and *yud*, which has a value of 10.

**48. (b)**    The shtreimel, sheitel (also spelled shaytel), and kipa are headcoverings. The gartle is a belt.

**49. (b)** The term *Chalitza* (sometimes spelled *Halitza*) means "removing [the shoe]." The widow removes her brother-in-law's shoe and says, "So shall be done to the man who will not build his brother's house."

**50. (a)** *Chupa*, sometimes spelled hupah, means "covering."

**51. (c, f)** are used primarily by Ashkenazim. The others are used by Sephardim.

**52. (c)** The Hebrew words mean "on high" or "to the heights."

**53. (b)** The words *El malay rachamim*, mean "God full of mercy." For short, the prayer is referred to as the *Malay*.

**54. (a)** The mezuza is placed on the right doorpost, one-third from the top. It is positioned at an angle of about 30 degrees, with the top of the mezuza leaning toward the interior of the room as one enters.

**55. (b)** People on their deathbed often recite a *Viddui* prayer.

**56. (b)** The actual Hebrew phrase is chillul Ha-Shem. Kiddush Ha-Shem ("sanctification of the Name") has the opposite meaning.

**57. (a)**  The word *mashgiach* ("watchman") is sometimes confused with *mashiach*, meaning "messiah."

**58. (b)**  These traditional Jewish foods were once very popular in Eastern Europe.

**59. (c)**  *Shalosh se'udot* means "three meals." On the Sabbath, Jews eat three meals. The third meal is called *se'uda shelishit*, of which *shaleshudis* is a distorted form.

**60. (c)**  American Orthodox Jews often referred to someone as FFB or "frum from birth," as contrasted with a person who turned to religion in later life.

**61. (b)**  *Gabbaim* is the plural form. Similar appointees stand alongside the Torah reader and prompt him if necessary.

**62. (a)**  Rabbi Judah Lowe ben Bezalel of Prague created such a creature. The word *golem* is used in Jewish literature to describe a stupid person.

**63. (a, d)**  *Zichrono li-veracha* is generally reserved for a distinguished person or scholar. *Alav ha-shalom* means "may he rest in peace."

**64. (b)**  The sashlike belt worn by chassidim to separate the lower (more mundane) part of the body from the upper (more spiritual) part is also called a gartle.

**65. (c)** *Shechina* is derived from the Hebrew root meaning "to dwell," implying God's omnipresence.

**66. (c)** *Meturgeman* is an Aramaic word meaning "translator" or "interpreter."

**67. (d)** The hora is danced at many Jewish weddings and celebrations and is particularly popular in Israel.

**68. (a)** Literally *yamim tovim* means "good days"; *mo'adim* means "appointed days"; and *chaggim* means "joyous days."

**69. (a)** In the vernacular, the three words are sometimes pronounced as if they are one word.

**70. (b)** Kaddish, introduced about one thousand years ago as a prayer for mourners, expresses one's faith in God.

**71. (b)** This modern Hebrew term means "I hope to see you again soon."

**72. (c)** The literal meaning of *Masora* is "that which has been transmitted."

**73. (a)** The Yiddish word *kugel* is derived from the German term meaning "globe" or "sphere."

**74. (c)**    From the German Koch, meaning "cook," and *Leffl*, meaning "spoon," a *kochleffl* is a long wooden spoon used to stir food while it is being cooked.

**75. (d)**    *Lamed* has a numerical value of 30 and *vav* of 6, totaling 36. The legend is recorded in the tractate Sukkah(45b).

**76. (b)**    *Lekach tov*, a biblical phrase (Proverbs 4:2) meaning "good teaching," refers to the sweet teachings of the Torah. Honey cake is served on Rosh Hashana.

**77. (d)**    These refer to types of prayer services that are conducted in various localities. Ashkenaz refers to Germanic countries, Polin to Poland, and Sefarad to Spain.

**78. (a)**    The term *letz* is found in the Book of Proverbs (14:6).

**79. (b, c, d)**    The letters *dalet*, *hay*, or *yud* followed by a diagonal diacritical mark are popularly used as an abbreviation for God's name.

**80. (a)**    Nordau called such Jews *Luftmenschen* (singular, *Luftmensch*), literally "men of the air."

**81. (d)**    The Hebrew word *kipa* was first used in the Talmud (Chulin 138a) to describe the woolen headcovering worn by the High Priest. *Koppel* is a Yiddish word for headcovering.

**82.** **(c)** *Yishuv* is a Hebrew word meaning "settlement."

**83.** **(c)** *Baruch ata* means "blessed art Thou."

**84.** **(b)** *Klezmer* is a Yiddish term derived from the two Hebrew words *klay zemer,* meaning "musical instrument." The instruments as well as the person playing them are called *klezmer.*

## Chapter 5
## Great Personalities

**1.** **(b)** Kissinger won the prize in 1973 and Begin in 1978. Fried, of Vienna, won it in 1911.

**2.** **(a)** Cardozo was appointed by President Herbert Hoover.

**3.** **(c)** Buchalter, known as Lepke, was reputed to be head of Murder, Inc. Siegel was nicknamed Bugsy.

**4.** **(c)** When Aaron of Lincoln died, his records showed that 430 people owed him 15,000 pounds. The English exchequer claimed all of his property.

**5.** **(c)** Cyrus Adler became president of the Jewish Theological Seminary of America.

6.  (a)  Akiba ben Joseph (Rabbi Akiba), who died in 135 C.E., was one of the great Rabbis of the Talmud. He was a supporter of Bar Kochba in his rebellion against Rome.

7.  (b, c)  Moses Alexander of Idaho and Arthur Seligman of New Mexico served as governors of their states. Javits was a senator from New York, and Koch was mayor of New York City.

8.  (c)  It is said that Alexander visited Jerusalem in 333 B.C.E. and was well received by the Jewish population.

9.  (a)  The Amoraim explained and commented on the teachings of earlier scholars whose rulings form the Mishna, the first part of the Talmud.

10.  (c)  He is often referred to as the Baal Shem Tov, meaning "Master of the Good Name."

11.  (c)  Bernard Baruch was a confidential advisor to Franklin D. Roosevelt and other presidents who succeeded him. He died in 1965.

12.  (a)  *The Travels of Benjamin of Tudela* was published posthumously in 1543. Tudela is a town in northern Spain.

13.  (a)  During his terms as premier, Mendès-France negotiated an armistice in Indochina.

**14. (b)** Beruria was the daughter of Chananya ben Teradyon, one of the Ten Martyrs put to death by the Romans for continuing to defy the law prohibiting the teaching of Torah to their students.

**15. (a)** The high point in Léon Blum's career was reached in 1936.

**16. (c)** Martin Buber died in 1965. Among his most famous works are *I and Thou*, *For the Sake of Heaven*, and *Tales of the Hasidim*.

**17. (b)** Ernest Bloch also wrote Avodat Ha-kodesh, musical renditions relating to the Sabbath service. Felix was a physicist, Ivan a German physician, and Joshua a librarian.

**18. (b, d)** Both were named Hannah.

**19. (a, b)** Both were named Moses.

**20. (b)** Jonas Salk discovered a polio vaccine that was to be administered by injection. In 1990, *Life* magazine included him as one of the one hundred most important Americans of the twentieth century.

**21. (d)** Milton Friedman (in 1976) and Paul Samuelson (in 1970) were Nobel Prize winners in economics.

**22. (c)**    The inhabitants of Chelm were known worldwide for their naiveté.

**23. (b)**    Reference to him is found in the talmudic tractate Taanit(3:8). His surname means "the encircler."

**24. (b)**    Disraeli, who died in 1881, was nevertheless a proud Jew. He was a favorite of Queen Victoria.

**25. (a)**    The opposition to Fortas by Republican as well as southern Democratic senators was based on his having accepted a $20,000 fee in 1966 from a charitable foundation after having joined the Court. Originally appointed in 1965, Fortas resigned from the Court in May 1969.

**26. (a)**    Dubinsky, who retired in 1966, was an important influence in local and national politics for decades.

**27. (c)**    The author of many books, Eban is particularly known for *My People: The Story of the Jews* (1968).

**28. (a)**    Einstein was keenly interested in Israeli scientific institutions, especially the Hebrew University, of which he was a trustee. He donated his manuscripts on the theory of relativity to the university.

**29. (d)** In January 1952 her diary was published in English under the title *Anne Frank: The Diary of a Young Girl.*

**30. (b)** Frankfurter served as legal advisor to the Zionist delegation at the 1919 Paris Peace Conference. He died in 1965.

**31. (c)** Sigmund Freud, who introduced the concept of psychoanalysis, was born in 1856 in Vienna and died in London in 1939.

**32. (b)** Shabbetai Tzevi (or Zevi) attracted many followers when he announced, following the horror of the Chmielnicki massacres in 1648, that he would redeem Israel. In the end he evoked the wrath of the Turkish authorities and saved his life only by converting to Islam.

**33. (c)** Along with Jacob Barsimon, who arrived in New Amsterdam a few months earlier, Asser Levy battled for the right to perform guard duty rather than pay a special tax.

**34. (c)** Nelson Glueck (1900-1971) is the author of *Rivers in the Desert*, a book about explorations in the Negev.

**35. (d)** In 1973, Gershwin was the last to be so honored.

**36. (d)** From 1892 until his death in 1901 Imber lived in the United States.

**37. (b)**    Yehuda Ha-Nasi, or Judah the Prince, was also honored with the title Rabbenu Ha-Kadosh, "Our Holy Teacher." The Mishna—the first part of the Talmud—was put in final written form in Palestine around 220 C.E.

**38. (b)**    Arthur Goldberg was also a U.S. Supreme Court Justice.

**39. (b)**    In August 1973 Richard Nixon appointed his national security advisor, Henry Kissinger, to replace William Rogers as secretary of state.

**40. (c)**    Jabotinsky was also a prolific writer of poetry and novels.

**41. (c)**    Of these six people, only Jonah is mentioned in the Bible. Hence, he lived first.

**42. (b)**    Littauer was a U.S. congressional representative from New York State.

**43. (c)**    In 1948 the U.S. government issued a commemorative postage stamp honoring Rabbi Goode.

**44. (a)**    Bela Schick discovered the test for diphtheria.

**45. (c)**    Ludwig Lewisohn achieved distinction as a professor of German at Ohio State University from 1911 to 1948. From 1948 until his death, he was professor of comparative literature at Brandeis University. Among his most famous works are *The Island Within* and *The Last Days of Shylock*.

**46. (c)**    Herbert H. Lehman was born in 1878 and died in 1963.

**47. (b)**    Rabbi Moses (Moshe) ben Maimon was better known as Maimonides, from the Greek meaning "son of Maimon."

**48. (b)**    The book *Cast a Giant Shadow* is the story of Marcus's life. The character of Marcus was portrayed by Kirk Douglas in a film made from the book.

**49. (c)**    The term Crypto-Jews applies to those Jews who adopted another religion under compulsion.

**50. (b)**    Golda Meir was chosen to succeed Levi Eshkol as prime minister in 1969 and was reelected at the end of 1973. She retired in 1974 and died in 1978.

**51. (c)**    Of all false messiahs, Shabbetai Tzevi (1626-1676) of Turkey, not mentioned here, was the most notorious.

**52. (c)**    Amos and Zechariah were prophets, and each has a book in the Bible named after him. Rashi was a French Bible commentator who lived about 1,500 years later.

**53. (a)**    These men were all great physicists. Michelson, an American, won the prize in 1907. Rabi, an American, won the prize in 1944. Segre, an Italian, won the prize in 1959.

**54. (c)**    Peres arrived in Palestine in 1934 at age eleven. In his younger years he worked closely with David Ben-Gurion.

**55. (c)**    Pulitzer was owner of *The St. Louis Post-Dispatch* and later *The New York World*. He represented a New York district in Congress in 1885. Pulitzer's father was Jewish, but his mother was Catholic.

**56. (b)**    Ramban (1194-c.1270) is an acronym for Rabbi Moses ben Nachman. He is often confused with Rambam (Maimonides), the twelfth-century scholar.

**57. (a)**    Yigael Yadin (1917-1984) is the soldier-scholar who was an expert on the Dead Sea Scrolls. He later served in the Knesset.

**58. (a)**    Abraham Ribicoff served as governor of Connecticut from 1955 to 1961 and as a U.S. senator from 1963 to 1981.

**59. (c)** Rickover was awarded the Medal of Freedom by President Jimmy Carter in 1980. He retired from the U.S. Navy in 1982 and died in 1986.

**60. (b)** In 1920 he organized the *Lehrhaus* in Frankfurt, Germany, which became a center of Jewish education for assimilated Jews eager to learn about their tradition.

**61. (a)** His five sons established offices in London, Paris, Vienna, Naples, and Frankfurt.

**62. (a)** In 1971 Sabin was awarded the United States Medal of Science. He died in 1993.

**63. (c)** Haym Salomon was born in 1740 and died in 1785.

**64. (a)** Their disciples were known as the School of Hillel and the School of Shammai.

**65. (a)** Spinoza was born in 1632 and died in 1677. He withdrew from Jewish society but never converted to another faith.

**66. (c)** Charles Steinmetz's middle name was Proteus. He died in 1923.

**67. (b)** Wallenberg was a Swedish diplomat stationed in Hungary.

**68. (c)**    Avraham Stern, whose pseudonym was Yair, was the head of the Stern Gang—the most militant anti-British group of the 1940s. Isaac Stern is a virtuoso violinist. Otto Stern, a physicist, was research professor of physics at the Carnegie Institute of Technology in Pittsburgh, Pennsylvania. William Stern was a German psychologist.

**69. (c)**    In 1929, together with Nahman Avigad, Sukenik discovered the mosaic floor of the sixth century C.E. synagogue at Bet Alpha in the Valley of Jezreel in Palestine.

**70. (a)**    Wasserman's famous test for diagnosing syphilis is commonly known as the Wasserman Reaction.

**71. (a)**    Goldberg resigned in 1965 at the request of President Lyndon Johnson so that he might become the U.S. ambassador to the United Nations.

**72. (a)**    Moses Maimonides was a famous Spanish scholar, philosopher, and physician.

**73. (d)**    Brandeis was appointed by President Wilson in 1916 and served until 1939. William Howard Taft, who was president of the U.S. from 1909 to 1913, was appointed by President Harding in 1921, and served till 1930.

**74. (c)** Herzl was called "Father of Political Zionism." In 1948, Weizmann was elected the first president of Israel.

**75. (b)** Cyrus, king of Persia, allowed the exiled Jews to return to Palestine.

**76. (b)** The shooting was witnessed by millions of television viewers. Ruby's rabbi was Hillel Silverman.

**77. (b)** It was not until 1948 that Israel actually became an independent state.

**78. (b)** Jacob Barsimon is reputed to have been the first Jewish settler in the entire New World.

**79. (a)** Ben-Zvi, whose original name was Shimshelevitz, published papers on several aspects of Jewish history, especially on the Samaritans and Oriental communities.

**80. (a)** A Jewish terrorist organization known as the Stern Gang, a splinter group of Lehi, claimed responsibility for Bernadotte's assassination.

**81. (d)** Just before the Six-Day War, Dayan joined the government as minister of defense. He resigned in 1974 amid criticism of his performance during the Yom Kippur War.

**82. (b)**    Dreyfus was unjustly accused of selling military secrets to the Germans. Clemenceau's journal was *L'Aurore*.

**83. (d)**    From 1950 to 1959 Eban also served as the Israeli ambassador to the United States.

**84. (c)**    He served as president for two terms and was succeeded by Ezer Weizman. Herzog was born in Ireland, where his father served as chief rabbi.

**85. (d)**    Brandeis and Cardozo were the other two Jewish justices who served on the Supreme Court at the same time.

**86. (c)**    Rebecca is believed to have been the prototype for Sir Walter Scott's Rebecca in *Ivanhoe*.

**87. (b)**    After the Nazi rise to power, Henrietta Szold became the leader of Youth Aliyah, which saved many thousands of Jewish boys and girls from extinction in Europe. She was always deeply interested in fostering friendly relationships between the Jews and Arabs of Palestine.

**88. (a)**    Russ Feingold and Herb Kohl were both elected to the U.S. Senate from Wisconsin in 1992.

**89. (a)** Holofernes was an Assyrian army commander who invaded Judea. The story is told in the Book of Judith.

**90. (c)** Under Joshua, the waters of the Jordan split as the Children of Israel crossed over in the area near Jericho. See the Book of Joshua, chapter 3.

**91. (c)** Uriah P. Levy was at the forefront of the battle to abolish corporal punishment in the U.S. Navy.

**92. (b)** Although a Jew by birth, Luis de Torres was baptized immediately before Columbus's expedition set sail.

**93. (d)** Earlier he served as a state senator. Many other Jews served in the U.S. Senate, but Lieberman was the first one who was avowedly Orthodox.

**94. (a)** Rabbi Kook established a yeshiva which became known as Merkaz Ha-rav.

**95. (d)** Kollek's autobiography, written in 1978, is entitled *For Jerusalem*. In 1993 he ran once again for reelection and lost to the Likud candidate, Ehud Olmert.

**96. (c)** Manasseh ben Israel was the Dutch rabbi. The Jews had been expelled from England in 1290 and were readmitted in 1655.

**97. (b)** Mordecai Manuel Noah was an American diplomat and author. He served as the United States consul to Tunis from 1813 to 1815 and later became sheriff of New York County.

**98. (d)** His Hebrew name was Yoseph ben Mattityahu Ha-Kohen. Flavius was the family name of Vespasian and his son Titus, who were the Roman rulers during Josephus's lifetime.

**99. (c, d)** Among others mentioned in (a) and (b), only Navon served as president. The other president not mentioned here is Shneour Zalman Shazar, the third president of Israel. Ezer Weizman succeeded Herzog.

**100. (c)** Even after Shabbetai Tzevi converted, not all of his followers abandoned him.

**101. (c)** The Geniza fragments were discovered in a special room in a synagogue in Fostat (Old Cairo), Egypt.

**102. (b)** Dianne Feinstein and Barbara Boxer of California were both elected in 1992.

**103. (a)** In 1986 Sharansky was finally released from prison and exchanged in Berlin for prisoners held by the West. His memoir is entitled *Fear No Evil* (1988).

**104. (a)** Sobel was an associate of Julius and Ethel Rosenberg, who were executed in 1953 for spying for the Soviet Union. Pollard spied for Israel and was arrested in November 1985.

**105. (a)** On the ninth day of Av in 70 C.E., Titus occupied the Temple Mount and set the Second Temple afire, burning it to the ground.

**106. (d)** Ginsburg was appointed by President Bill Clinton in 1993. Bella Abzug was once a member of Congress. Feinstein and Boxer were elected U.S. senators in 1992.

**107. (b)** Hungarian-born Hanna Szenes (Senesh) left her comfortable home in Budapest in 1939 to help rebuild Palestine as a national homeland. She was captured by the Nazis, and after standing trial in Budapest, was executed.

**108. (b)** In 1497, five years after their explusion from Spain, the Jews were expelled from Portugal by order of King Manuel.

**109. (d)** Yochanan ben Zakkai was so treated because he had been a proponent of pacifism toward Rome. The year permission was granted is presumed to be 68 C.E.

**110. (c)**    Golda Meir was prime minister of Israel. Henrietta Szold was not a social worker by profession, although she did a good deal of important work in that field. Rebekah Kohut was active in the National Council of Jewish Women.

**111. (c)**    Chaim Weizmann pursued his studies at German and Swiss universities and was later appointed lecturer in biological chemistry at Manchester University, England. In 1916 he became director of the British Admiralty Chemical Laboratories.

## Chapter 6
## The Jewish Community

**1. (a)**    Karaites accepted the Bible literally but rejected the talmudic interpretations of the Rabbis.

**2. (b)**    *B'nai b'rith*, meaning "sons of the covenant," refers to the covenant Abraham made with God as described in Genesis 12 and confirmed in Deuteronomy 29.

**3. (a)**    The Red Cross has not recognized Magen David Adom as it has similar organizations in other countries. The Red Crescent is the Moslem equivalent of the Red Cross.

4. **(a)** Although Rabbi Wise was a Zionist, the American Jewish Congress received financial support from non-Zionists as well.

5. **(c)** The American Jewish Committee was founded in New York in the aftermath of the 1903 Kishinev (Bessarabia) pogrom. Jacob Schiff and Oscar S. Straus were among the founding fathers.

6. **(c)** The Council's first president was Lessing J. Rosenwald. After the 1967 Six-Day War many of its leaders and supporters abandoned the organization.

7. **(a)** The cities of Sura and Pumbedita were located in Babylonia (present-day Iraq) during the first ten centuries C.E. Many of the greatest Jewish academies of learning were housed in these cities.

8. **(a)** Bar-Ilan University, located on the outskirts of Tel Aviv, was organized under Orthodox auspices.

9. **(c)** David Ben-Gurion was Israel's first prime minister. After his retirement he settled in S'deh Boker, in the Negev.

10. **(a)** The name of the organization is WIZO (Women's International Zionist Organization). Its counterpart in America is Hadassah.

11. (a)    At this meeting, held in Basle, Switzerland, Theodor Herzl was elected president of this world Zionist organization.

12. (a)    The organization is named after the famous Rabbi Hillel of the first century B.C.E. Hillel provides full-time and part-time rabbis and other professionals who tend to the religious, educational, and social needs of Jewish students.

13. (c)    The school is named after the biblical Bezalel, a craftsman who was selected by God to build the Tabernacle which accompanied the Israelites during their march through the desert. See Exodus 35:30.

14. (a)    Because of their service, *Hofjuden* (a German word) were accorded special privileges.

15. (a)    Hebrew Union College was organized in 1875 by Rabbi Isaac M. Wise to train Reform rabbis.

16. (c)    In 1932 it organized Youth Aliyah, a program to resettle and train Jewish youth in Palestine. By 1970 it had resettled 125,000 Jewish children in Israel.

17. (b) These were a type of oracular device placed inside the breastplate worn by Aaron, the High Priest. See Exodus 28:30 and Leviticus 8:8. The exact meaning of the words is uncertain. Some scholars believe that *urim* and *tumim* mean "light" and "completeness" respectively.

18. (a) The Hebrew quote from which the acronym is formed is *Bet Yaakov l'chu ve-nelcha*.

19. (c) President Woodrow Wilson appointed Brandeis in 1916, and Brandeis served on the Court until his retirement in 1939.

20. (a) Chabad is an acronym formed from the first letters of the Hebrew words *chochma*, *bina*, and *deah*, meaning "wisdom, understanding, and knowledge."

21. (a) In 1922 Rabbi Kaplan founded the Society for the Advancement of Judaism. His magnum opus is *Judaism as a Civilization*.

22. (b) Dr. Belkin became the second president of Yeshiva University. Norman Lamm succeeded Belkin.

23. (a) The flag of Israel has a white background with blue stripes. The designer had a talit (prayershawl) in mind when he created the design.

**24. (c)**   A Chevra Kadisha is a group that handles the details of burial. The words mean "holy society."

**25. (c)**   Billions of dollars have been raised since World War II to assist in settling refugees and other newcomers to Israel.

**26. (a)**   Viscount Peel was chairman of the Royal Commission that recommended the division of Palestine into Arab and Jewish states.

**27. (b)**   HIAS stands for Hebrew Immigrant Aid Society. The more accurate name is Hebrew Sheltering and Immigrant Aid Society. It was created in 1909 by the merger of the Hebrew Sheltering House Association (founded in 1884) and the Hebrew Immigrant Aid Society (founded in 1902).

**28. (a)**   Rabbi Kahane was assassinated in 1990 in New York City by an Arab terrorist.

**29. (a)**   The United Synagogue of America was founded in 1913 by Solomon Schechter, president of the Jewish Theological Seminary.

**30. (b)**   Moses Dropsie accepted Judaism at age fourteen and remained a devout Jew. Cyrus Adler was the first president of what is now called Dropsie University but was originally known as College for Hebrew and Cognate Learning.

31. (a)     Max Nordau, best known for his devotion to Zionism, was one of Herzl's advisors on Zionist problems.

32. (a)     The name was changed in 1956.

33. (d)     The words *Yad Va-shem*, which are taken from the Book of Isaiah (56:5), mean "a memorial and a name." There are many such Holocaust museums throughout the world.

34. (c)     The Sanhedrin convened by Napoleon met in Paris in February 1807 and consisted of eighty delegates including forty rabbis. It publicly condemned moneylending at high rates of interest.

35. (c)     These two organizations, arms of Reform Judaism, are related to the Union of American Hebrew Congregations.

36. (b)     The word *shul* evolved from the German word *Schule*, meaning "school," because the synagogue was also used as a house of study.

37. (a)     In 1980 Goldmann wrote a long article for the left-wing German weekly *Die Welt* in which he castigated Israel, calling it "a greater disaster than Auschwitz."

**38.** **(c)** The Pharisees were closer to the people, and their influence was more enduring. They maintained that the Bible is subject to interpretation, as proposed by the Rabbis of the Talmud.

**39.** **(c)** In 1958, on the occasion of its fortieth anniversary, Habimah was officially recognized as the National Theatre of Israel.

**40.** **(c)** *Ulpan* means "study." Its plural form is *ulpanim*. Today, many such schools exist throughout Israel.

**41.** **(b)** *Bet din* (a court of law) is closely related to Sanhedrin. The Sanhedrin was a Jewish high tribunal in the postbiblical period.

**42.** **(a)** In 1948 the Haganah became the nucleus of the Israel Defense Forces, Israel's regular army.

**43.** **(a)** Its military framework was completely dismantled in 1948 when the State of Israel was established. Its Hebrew name was Irgun Tzeva'i Le'umi and its acronym was Etzel.

**44.** **(c)** The Rabbi Isaac Elchanan Theological Seminary is the rabbinical school of Yeshiva University.

**45.** **(b)** The funds were used to buy land in Palestine by the Jewish National Fund. The blue charity box was called a *pushke* in Yiddish.

**46. (c)** The pilgrims of whom the Bible speaks were those Jews who visited the Temple in Jerusalem during the three major festivals.

**47. (a)** Youth Aliyah was responsible for saving thousands of Jewish European children. From 1933 to 1945 Youth Aliyah was headed by Henrietta Szold, one of the founders of Hadassah.

**48. (a)** Their capital was Samaria, hence the name Samaritans. They are called Shomronim in Hebrew. The Talmud, in which Samaritans do not believe, refers to the sect as Kutim. Small communities of Samaritans still exist in Tel Aviv and Nablus.

**49. (c)** Workmen's Circle actively assisted in the formation of unions in the needle and other trades in which Jewish immigrants were pioneers.

**50. (c)** Vladimir Jabotinsky and Joseph Trumpeldor were the Jewish leaders who proposed the idea of a Jewish legion.

**51. (a)** Planting trees was a much later project of the Jewish National Fund.

**52. (b)** Of this group, only Cyrus Adler was not a rabbi.

**53. (c)** JWB stands for Jewish Welfare Board(or, more accurately, National Jewish Welfare Board). In 1990 the name of the organization was changed to Jewish Community Centers of North America. Its Commission on Jewish Chaplaincy certifies rabbinic candidates for the military chaplaincy.

**54. (c)** Magnes served for four years as rabbi of New York's Temple Emanuel. In 1921 he settled in Palestine and in 1925 was elected chancellor of Hebrew University.

**55. (d)** The Knesset, or Parliament, of Israel consists of 120 members and most closely resembles the House of Commons in its manner of conducting governmental affairs.

**56. (c)** This labor party was created in 1930 through the merger of Ha-poel Hatzair and Ahdut Ha-avoda. In the 1959 election Mapai received 55.43% of the votes. After the 1967 Six-Day War, Mapai, Ahdut Ha-Avoda, and Rafi merged to form the Israel Labor Party, with fifty-five parliamentary seats.

**57. (c)** The Second Temple was destroyed in the year 70 C.E. by the Romans, when Titus took command of the Roman army from his father, Vespasian.

**58. (d)** Jonah B. Wise, who died in 1900, was Isaac M. Wise's son. He was also a rabbi.

**59. (a, d)**   These groups lived centuries apart and could not have been in direct conflict.

**60. (c)**   As of 1993 approximately sixty were Jews. In 1992 each Nobel Prize winner received $1.2 million.

**61. (a)**   Sixteen of the first forty Jewish Nobel Prize winners won the award for their achievements in medicine; thirteen for their achievements in physics.

**62. (b)**   While the words are associated with the Cross, the main goal of the Crusades, which began in 1096, was to free Palestine from the rule of the Moslem "infidels." En route through Europe, the Crusaders took the lives of many Jews who were also considered infidels.

**63. (a)**   The scheme was acceptable to Herzl but was rejected by members of the Zionist Congress.

**64. (a)**   *Karaite*, derived from the Hebrew, means "one who follows the Mikra [or Torah]" exclusively.

**65. (c)**   *Falasha* means "stranger" or "wanderer" in Ge'ez, an ancient Ethiopian dialect.

66. (a)     The order was known as Grant's Order #11. It stipulated that any Jew returning to the area would be arrested.

67. (d)     *Haganah* means "defense." In 1948, the Haganah became the nucleus of the Israel Defense Forces.

68. (b)     These Jews were known as Marranos, a Spanish word meaning "swine."

69. (d)     This applied even to those who had converted and were practicing Christians. These laws were known as the Nuremberg Laws.

## Chapter 7
## Significant Sites & Momentous Events

1. (a)      Other occupied territories were to be returned at a later date.

2. (c)      Treblinka and Majdanek were situated in Poland, Terezin in Czechoslovakia. There were a total of 1,634 Nazi concentration camps and satellites, and more than 900 labor camps.

3. (c)      *Auto de fe* is the Spanish form of the Portuguese *auto-da-fé*.

4. **(a)** Knowledge of the massacre was kept secret until the Soviet poet Yevgeni Yevtushenko wrote his famous poem *Babi Yar*.

5. **(b)** The Roman rulers sent fourteen Procurators to rule Judea over a sixty-year period.

6. **(c)** Beersheba is the biblical southern city (see Judges 20:1 for the reference). Eilat is also mentioned but is not referred to as the southern boundary.

7. **(b)** An individual who comes to live in Israel is granted automatic citizenship if his or her mother is Jewish or if he or she has converted to Judaism and does not profess another religion.

8. **(a)** S'deh Boker is in the Negev, in the south of Israel.

9. **(a)** The best known cases of these unfounded blood accusations are those of Hugh of Lincoln(1255) and Simon of Trent(1475).

10. **(c)** The first large shipment consisting of 10,000 Jews arrived at Buchenwald in November 1938. The camp was liberated by American troops on April 11, 1945, freeing some 21,000 survivors.

11. **(b)** Camp David, in Maryland, is the U.S. presidential retreat.

**12. (b)**    The Germans established very few camps in Germany; most were in other countries, especially Poland.

**13. (b)**    Five times as salty as the ocean, the Dead Sea is called Yam Ha-melach ("Salt Sea") in Hebrew.

**14. (c)**    The Intifada subsided after the signing of the 1993 peace accord between Israel and the PLO.

**15. (c)**    The wall fell after the Priests blew one final long blast.

**16. (c)**    The Dead Sea Scrolls are on exhibit in Jerusalem in the Shrine of the Book, a building which is part of the Israel Museum.

**17. (a)**    During that period almost one hundred Jews were killed and 1,300 synagogues desecrated.

**18. (a)**    As a result of Luther's revolution, the condition of the Jews became markedly worse. At first, Luther spoke favorably of the Jews, condemning their mistreatment by the Catholic Church. He hoped that they would be attracted to his views, but when they rejected them, he encouraged persecution of the Jews in Germany.

**19. (b)** When the Romans broke into the fortress atop Masada, they found 960 dead people, including the rebel leader Eleazar ben Yair.

**20. (a)** These laws, enacted during the month of May, were largely responsible for the wholesale emigration of Jews from Russia during that period.

**21. (b)** Affirmative action is the opposite of the quota system known as numerus clausus.

**22. (c)** Israeli troops stormed the school. As a consequence, twenty children, one Israeli soldier, and three terrorists were killed.

**23. (b)** Babylonia is today known as Iraq.

**24. (b)** The documents were called *Protocols of the Elders of Zion*. The group circulating them persuaded Henry Ford to support them financially. The auto magnate later regretted his action.

**25. (b)** According to legend, the Sambatyon was the river the Ten Tribes crossed when they were exiled from Babylonia by the Assyrians in 719 B.C.E.

**26. (c)** The trials, which ended on October 16, 1946, are known as the Nuremberg Trials. Eleven Nazis were found guilty and sentenced to be hanged.

**27.** **(c)** The Israelis attacked Egypt on October 29, 1956 in order to break the ring of encirclement created by the anti-Israel alliance of Egypt, Jordan, and Syria. France and England had come to the aid of Israel by bombing strategic Egyptian positions, but the pressure brought to bear by the United States caused France and England to withdraw, and Israel had to evacuate the Gaza Strip, which it had captured.

**28.** **(b)** The Yemenites, who had never before flown in an airplane, believed the airlift to be the fulfillment of the biblical statement, "I bore you on the wings of eagles and brought you to me"(Exodus 19:4).

**29.** **(b)** Between 1948 and 1967 these buildings could not be used becuase they were in a United Nations-supervised neutral zone between Israel and Jordan.

**30.** **(c)** These scenes symbolize the humiliation to which the Jews were subjected after the Second Temple was destroyed by the Romans in 70 C.E.

**31.** **(a)** The Polish name of Auschwitz is Oświeçim; in Yiddish it is called Ushpitzin.

**32.** **(a, d)** Bethlehem is the city in which King David was born and also the native city of Naomi, mother-in-law of Ruth.

**33. (b)** Aside from Pumbedita, the other major center of learning in Babylonia was Nehardea. Babylonia is in present-day Iraq.

**34. (b)** Of the 20,000 Jews who went to Birobidzhan in the early days of the experiment, 11,000 had left by 1934. In 1991 its Jewish population was 6,500.

**35. (a)** Canaan is mentioned several times in the Book of Genesis as a personal name and a place name. See Genesis 28:8 and 36:2.

**36. (a)** The large depository of old sacred books was called Geniza, meaning "hiding" in Hebrew.

**37. (b)** It is known as the Mosque of Omar because it was built, in 738, to replace the temporary structure that had been erected a century earlier by Calif Omar. It is considered to be the third holiest site in Islam.

**38. (d)** Galilee is a form of the Hebrew word *galil*, meaning "round, rolling." Some of the major cities in the Galilee are Tiberias, Haifa, and Safed.

**39. (d)** In the Venetian-Italian dialect, *ghetto* means "iron foundry." In later years, all areas to which Jews were confined were called ghettos.

**40. (c)** It was captured during the 1967 Six-Day War.

**41. (a)**    Haifa, Tiberias, and Acre are in the northern part of Israel.

**42. (b)**    The country we call Iran today is the Persia of old. As of 1994 approximately 75,000 Jews were living there.

**43. (b)**    These cities are mentioned in the Book of Exodus (1:11).

**44. (b)**    The Touro Synagogue, a small quaint structure, is located in Newport, Rhode Island.

**45. (c)**    Between July 23, 1942 and August 28, 1942, the first five weeks of operation, 312,500 Jews, including 245,000 from Warsaw, were deported to Treblinka.

**46. (c)**    She died near Bethlehem after giving birth to Benjamin.

**47. (b)**    The burial place of Moses was kept unknown so future generations would not be tempted to deify him.

## Chapter 8
# The Literary Scene

**1. (c)**    Yael's father was Moshe Dayan. Ruth was the name of Yael Dayan's mother.

2. **(b)** In 1966 Agnon was awarded the Nobel Prize for Literature.

3. **(c)** He succeeded Solomon Schechter at Cambridge as a lecturer in Talmud and taught there until his death in 1925.

4. **(d)** Her short stories "The Shawl" (1980) and "Rosa (1983) appeared in *The New Yorker* magazine.

5. **(c)** The Passover Haggadah has appeared in more than 3,500 editions over the past two thousand years.

6. **(d)** Her original first name was Leonie. Sachs was born in Germany in 1891 but immigrated to Sweden in 1940. She died there in 1970.

7. **(b)** Asher Ginsberg was opposed to Herzl's idea of a Jewish political state in Palestine, favoring instead a spiritual center.

8. **(c)** Asch's aim in writing books on Christian themes was to demonstrate the common heritage of Jews and Christians. Orthodox Jewish circles, in particular, did not look with favor upon his writings.

9. **(b)** When he wrote *Love Story*, Segal was a professor of classics at Yale University.

**10.  (c)**    Besides Saul Bellow's famous novel *The Adventures of Augie March*, he wrote *Herzog* and *Humboldt's Gift* (for which he won the Nobel Prize for Literature in 1976).

**11.  (b)**    Salo Baron also wrote *The Russian Jews Under Tsars and Soviets* (1964). Born in 1895, Baron died in 1989.

**12.  (b)**    Cohen taught at the City College of New York from 1912 to 1938.

**13.  (c)**    The Rabbis forbade the use of Elisha ben Avuya's proper name, and he was given the name Acher, meaning "the other one."

**14.  (b)**    He is also the author of *Spartacus* and the bestseller *The Immigrant*.

**15.  (c)**    Cassuto's Italian name was Umberto. Early in his career he was professor of Hebrew language and literature at the University of Florence.

**16.  (d)**    In many respects it is like the Book of Proverbs, containing many wise sayings and teachings.

**17.  (a)**    Eliezer ben Yehudah is also renowned for his founding, in 1888, of the Hebrew Language Council, which encouraged the use of Hebrew as a spoken language.

**18.** **(d)** In 1959 his book was acclaimed as a master-piece of Holocaust literature, bringing him France's leading literary award.

**19.** **(a)** Nachmanides and Mendelssohn were also great scholars. *The Mishneh Torah* of Maimonides is more widely studied than his *Guide.*

**20.** **(a)** Benjamin of Tudela began traveling about 1165. His book describes his travels to France, Italy, Greece, Syria, Palestine, Iraq, the Persian Gulf, Egypt, and Sicily.

**21.** **(c)** He is also author of *The Tales of Rabbi Nachman of Bratslav* (1972) and *The Legend of the Baal Shem* (1969).

**22.** **(a)** Bialik's famous poem about a yeshiva student is called *Ha-matmid* [or *Ha-masmid*, the Ashkenazic pronunciation]. *Ir Ha-harega* and *Megillat* [or *Megillas*] *Ha-esh* are two of his many other poems.

**23.** **(d)** The *Mishneh Torah* of Maimonides (also known as Rambam) contains fourteen sections and is also called *Yad* [having a numerical value of fourteen] *Ha-chazaka.*

**24.** **(c)** Zweig died in 1942.

**25.** **(c)** Five years after he came to America he was hired as a police reporter for the *New York Commercial Advertiser*, edited by Lincoln Steffens.

**26. (b)**    Franz Werfel spent the last years of his life as an Orthodox Jew.

**27. (b)**    The actual author of this bible of the kabbalists is Moses de Leon, a thirteenth-century Spanish mystic. The Zohar is essentially a commentary on the Five Books of Moses, Song of Songs, Ruth, and Lamentations.

**28. (c)**    His son, Eli, a professor of economics at Columbia University beginning in 1935, wrote *Keeper of the Law*, a biography of his father.

**29. (c)**    The Dead Sea Scrolls were found in September 1947 by Bedouins in various locations west of the Dead Sea. The Shrine of the Book was erected in 1965.

**30. (a)**    *Gentleman's Agreement* became a bestseller and was quickly adapted to the screen. It won an Academy Award as best movie of the year.

**31. (a, b, c)**    are all correct answers.

**32. (b)**    Her *Feminine Mystique* (1963) is considered the most important book on the history of the women's (feminist) movement.

**33. (a)**    Hyamson and Schechter also taught at the Jewish Theological Seminary. Schechter served as president as well.

**34. (c)** Born in 1821, Pinsker was a Russian physician who wrote his pamphlet after observing the pogroms in Odessa in 1882. *Auto-Emancipation* was written in German.

**35. (b)** He won the Pulitzer Prize in 1949 for *Death of a Salesman*.

**36. (c)** Talmud is the inclusive name for both the Mishna and the Gemara.

**37. (a)** He also resided in several Christian and Moslem towns, principally Cordova (Cordoba), the hometown of Maimonides.

**38. (d)** Since 1972 Abraham B. Yehoshua has taught at Haifa University. He is a winner of the prestigious Israel Prize for Literature.

**39. (a)** He is also author of *Topaz* and *QB VII*.

**40. (a)** Her book, *The Memoirs of Glückel of Hameln*, is a source for much of what is known about Jewish history and culture in Central Europe in the seventeenth and eighteenth centuries.

**41. (b)** Golden is best remembered for his essay entitled "Vertical Integration," which suggested that all seats be removed from restaurant counters so that whites would not have to sit with blacks when eating.

**42. (b)** Safire wrote *Before the Fall* (1975) as well as books on language and literature.

**43. (a)** Samuel Loeb Gordon (1867-1933), a Hebrew author and Bible commentator, is better known by the acronym Shalag.

**44. (a)** Early in his career Graetz was a lecturer in Jewish history at Breslau University.

**45. (d)** Based on Mailer's wartime experiences, the work was hailed as the finest U.S. novel to come out of World War II.

**46. (c)** His two succeeding memoir-novels, entitled *Dawn* (1961) and *The Accident* (1962), complete the trilogy. *The Jews of Silence* describes his 1965 visit to the Soviet Union.

**47. (b)** For many years, beginning in 1965, Potok was editor of the Jewish Publication Society of America.

**48. (b)** In 1929 he published *Crescas' Critique of Aristotle*.

**49. (b)** Wouk was born in New York City in 1915. He won the Pulitzer Prize for *The Caine Mutiny*.

**50. (c)** Heschel, an activist, marched with Martin Luther King in a 1965 freedom walk.

51. **(a)**  Next to Bialik, Tchernichovsky was probably the greatest Hebrew poet of his time. He left Europe for Palestine in 1931.

52. **(c)**  Stone also wrote *The Agony and the Ecstasy*. His original name was Tennenbaum.

53. **(a)**  In 1978 he received the Nobel Prize for Literature.

54. **(d)**  Aimé Pallière was born in 1875 and died in 1949. *The Unknown Sanctuary* is his autobiography.

55. **(b)**  Imber's famous poem, Hatikvah, became Israel's national anthem.

56. **(d)**  Author and social critic Oz was born in 1939. In 1989 he wrote *To Know a Woman*, about a retired Israeli spy.

57. **(c)**  Brod ignored Kafka's request.

58. **(c)**  *The New Colossus* is inscribed on the Statue of Liberty, which was a gift to the United States from France.

59. **(a)**  Born in Austria in 1831, Brentano started the important bookstore that carries his name. He died in 1886.

**60. (b)** The book reveals Pasternak's estrangement from Judaism.

**61. (c)** Zangwill also tried his hand as a playwright, authoring *The Melting Pot*. He died in 1926.

**62. (b)** It is believed that Rebecca Gratz (1781-1869) was the prototype for Sir Walter Scott's heroine in *Ivanhoe*.

**63. (d)** Stein's autobiographical study describes her life as an expatriot.

**64. (a)** All worked for *The Washington Post* during their careers.

**65. (d)** Kazin offers a graphic description of his generation, which came of age in the Jewish neighborhoods of the 1930s.

**66. (a)** His best known book in the field, *Major Trends in Jewish Mysticism*, has become a classic.

**67. (c)** After Ribalow's death, the weekly became a bimonthly publication. Menachem's son, Harold, was also a journalist and author.

**68. (b)** His name is Karl Marx. Alexander Marx was a Jewish historian. Adolph Marx was a Jewish composer. Groucho Marx was, of course, the popular comedian.

**69.  (b)**    *Fiddler*, which originally starred Zero Mostel, was written by Joseph Stein, with music by Jerry Bock and lyrics by Sheldon Harnick. The musical is based on the character Tevye der Milchiger (Tevye the Milkman) in one of his novels.

**70.  (d)**    Josephus was commander of the Jewish stronghold Jutapata, in Western Galilee, which the Romans captured in 67 C.E.

**71.  (c)**    One of Peretz's early works was *Pictures of a Provincial Journey* (1891), in which he notes his impressions of Jewish shtetl life.

**72.  (a)**    Ozick is the recipient of many prestigious awards, including the Distinguished Service in Jewish Letters award from the Jewish Theological Seminary.

**73.  (c)**    Along with Sholom Aleichem and I. L. Peretz, Mendele was one of the great Yiddish writers of the past century.

**74.  (b)**    Ann Landers' birth name is Esther Friedman and Abigail's is Pauline Friedman. They were born in Sioux City, Iowa, in 1918. Abigail's column is entitled "Dear Abby."

**75.  (b)**    His original name was Opatovsky.

**76.  (a)**    Klausner, who died in 1958, was an authority on the Jewish history of the Second Temple period.

**77. (c)** Mapu's Hebrew work, written in 1853, was a romantic historical novel set in the biblical period of King Hezekiah. It was entitled *Ahavat Tziyon (Love of Zion)*.

**78. (c)** Sholom (sometimes spelled Sholem) Aleichem's real name was Shalom Rabinovich.

**79. (d)** *The Young Lions* is considered one of the finest novels of the post-World War II era and was adapted for the screen in 1958. *Bury the Dead* deals with a group of dead soldiers who refuse to be buried.

**80. (a)** In 1957 she won the prestigious Israel Prize for Education. Yeshayahu Leibowitz died in 1994.

**81. (c)** Most of Meyer Levin's books deal primarily with Israeli and Jewish life.

**82. (c)** His first novel was *City Boy*, written in 1948. In 1971 he wrote *The Winds of War* and in 1978 *War and Remembrance*.

**83. (a)** She was active in organizations such as the New York Urban League.

**84. (a)** Maurice Samuel was brought up in England and settled in the United States in 1914. He died in 1972.

**85.** **(a)** Malamud was a nonbeliever with a strong moral code. He also won the National Book Award in 1958 for *The Magic Barrel*, a collection of stories.

## Chapter 9
## Arts, Entertainment & Sports

**1.** **(b)** Schacht entertained fans before games and earned the title "Clown Prince of Baseball."

**2.** **(a)** Maurice Schwartz produced more than 150 plays by noted Jewish authors.

**3.** **(a)** Perlman made his official concert debut in a performance at New York's Carnegie Hall in 1963.

**4.** **(d)** Spitz set a new record in each of the seven swimming events in which he competed. In 1992, at the age of forty, he tried to make a comeback but failed to earn a place on the U.S. Olympic swimming team.

**5.** **(b)** Schor's art depicts Jewish life in Eastern Europe. He died in 1961.

**6.** **(d)** The movie produced by Spielberg is entitled *Schindler's List*. In addition to winning the 1993 Academy Award for best motion picture, it earned Spielberg the Best Director award.

7.  **(d)**      All won boxing titles.

8.  **(a)**      Gillman later became one of the leading pro coaches, heading such teams as the Los Angeles Rams and the Houston Oilers.

9.  **(a)**      Fleischer, who was born in 1887 and died in 1972, was an outstanding boxing promoter. He was often referred to as "Mr. Boxing."

10. **(a)**      In 1938 he hit 58 home runs. Greenberg is the first Jew to be named to the Baseball Hall of Fame. He is also a member of the Sports Hall of Fame in Israel.

11. **(b)**      Born in 1874, Kalich came to the United States in 1895.

12. **(c)**      The character of Baby Snooks, an impish girl, was modeled after the real-life child star Baby Peggy and became part of Brice's vaudeville act in 1912.

13. **(b)**      In 1956 Cantor won a special Academy Award for service.

14. **(c)**      Tucker's original name was Kalish. She called herself the "Last of the Red-hot Mamas."

**15. (c)**   Ernest Bloch was a composer of Jewish music. His works include *Israel Symphony*; *America*, written for chorus and orchestra; and Schelomo, a rhapsody for cello and orchestra. His *Avodat Ha-Kodesh, a* Sabbath service, was first performed in 1934.

**16. (d)**   Picon appeared in more than two hundred Yiddish productions and starred in the Broadway musical *Milk and Honey* in 1961. She played Yente the matchmaker in the film version of *Fiddler on the Roof*.

**17. (a)**   Dolph retired in 1963 and Danny retired in 1991.

**18. (a)**   His four consecutive home runs tied a Major League record.

**19. (b)**   Benny Friedman later played professionally for the New York Giants.

**20. (d)**   Franklin became one of Spain's leading matadors, reaching the zenith of his career in the early 1930s.

**21. (b)**   Sherry was born in 1935. His brother, Norm, was a Major League catcher.

**22. (d)**   Dyan Cannon was originally Samile Diane Friesen. Paulette Goddard was originally Marian Levee. Lily Palmer was originally Maria Peiser.

**23. (a)** They were all cantors, but Richard Tucker later became an opera singer.

**24. (a)** Howard Cosell was in the broadcast business for almost four decades.

**25. (a)** Epstein died in 1959.

**26. (d)** Koufax won the Cy Young Award three times and was elected to the Jewish Sports Hall of Fame.

**27. (c)** His show was called *The Milton Berle Show*.

**28. (d)** Abrahams won the 100-meter dash at the 1924 Paris Olympics.

**29. (b)** His original name was Jacob Gershvin. He died in 1937.

**30. (c)** After retiring, Grossman began to work full-time as an insurance executive with a Pittsburgh firm.

**31. (a)** Fischer is a member of a Christian sect. Spassky, a Russian Jew, is the man whom he beat in 1972 for the world championship.

**32. (c)** In 1888 the Adlers made their stage debut in America.

**33. (b)** The play, written by Ann Nichols in 1927, was produced on Broadway in 1937.

**34. (c)** He took the surname of his idol, Robert Houdini.

**35. (a)** He is also renowned for his Young People's Concerts and his *Kaddish* composition. Bernstein died in 1990.

**36. (c)** Gertrude Berg is best remembered for her portrayal of the character Mollie Goldberg on both radio and television.

**37. (d)** Bess Myerson, born in New York City in 1924, won the title in 1945.

**38. (a)** Stark was head coach of Dartmouth before and after World War II. He was born in 1867 and died in 1968.

**39. (c)** Zukor was born in Hungary in 1873 and died in 1976. At the 1948 Academy Awards he was honored for his contribution to the motion picture industry.

**40. (c)** Agam was born in 1928. After 1951, he spent much of his time in Paris. In 1993 he illustrated a Passover Haggadah in his unique style.

**41. (b)**     Rubinstein was born in Lodz, Poland, in 1887 and began his career at age twelve. A publicist dropped the *h* from Arthur's name "for effect," promoting him as Artur. Nonetheless, Rubinstein also signed his name Arthur.

**42. (c)**     Dick Savitt was the only male Jew ever to win Wimbledon. (Angela Buxton won the doubles in 1956.) Flam was ranked fourth in the world in 1967 and second in the United States in 1956 and 1957.

**43. (b)**     Hepzibah (also spelled Hephzibah or Cheftzi-ba) was the name of the wife of Hezekiah, king of Judah. See Second Kings 21:1.

**44. (a)**     Myer played second base.

**45. (b)**     Benny, born in Waukegan, Illinois, in 1894, was popular on radio and television. He died in 1974.

**46. (b)**     Auerbach coached the Boston Celtics.

**47. (b, d)**     Davis was the first black entertainer to convert to Judaism.

**48. (d)**     They lost all four times: in 1991, 1992, 1993, and 1994. Levy is a member of the Jewish Sports Hall of Fame.

**49. (b)** It was dubbed the first adult comic strip in America.

**50. (c)** In recent years he has become a spokesman for senior citizens.

**51. (b)** Steve Lawrence met Eydie Gormé on Steve Allen's *Tonight Show*.

**52. (c)** Of this group of four Jewish chess masters, only Reshevsky settled in the United States. He never won a world title, although he represented the U.S. in many international tournaments.

**53. (a)** Saperstein, who organized and coached the team, was elected to the Jewish Sports Hall of Fame in Israel.

**54. (c)** During his career, Slapsie Maxie Rosenbloom (so nicknamed by Damon Runyon becuase the boxer would often slap opponents with open gloves) won 208 fights. He is a member of the Boxing Hall of Fame.

**55. (b)** Jan Peerce was the brother-in-law of Richard Tucker. Tucker died in 1975. Peerce died in 1984.

**56. (b)** Gordon had a total of twenty-seven homers in 1950 when he hit .304 and drove in one hundred runs. In that year he hit four home runs with the bases full.

57. (a)    In 1969, together with Hal David, Bach-
           arach won an Academy Award for the song
           "Raindrops Keep Fallin' on My Head."

58. (a)    In 1942 Berlin won an Academy Award for
           the song "White Christmas," from *Holiday
           Inn*.

59. (c)    Originally, a fifth brother, Gummo, whose
           real name was Milton, was also part of the
           team.

60. (c)    This international Jewish sports festival was
           held under the auspices of the Maccabi
           World Union. Prior to 1932, competition
           was held in Czechoslovakia (1929) and Bel-
           gium (1931). The event is held every four
           years.

61. (c)    In the year Stone won the Cy Young Award,
           his record was 25-7.

62. (b)    Eddie Gottlieb, born in 1900, played for,
           managed, and owned the Philadelphia War-
           riors at various points in his career. Hen-
           shel, born in 1890, was prominent in ama-
           teur athletics. He managed the 92nd Street
           YMHA basketball team for a time, but
           gained real prominence as a member of the
           U.S. Olympic Basketball Committee, on
           which he served from its inception until his
           death in 1936.

**63.** **(a)** He also wrote dozens of other popular operettas.

**64.** **(b)** Max Baer's brother, Buddy, was also a boxer.

**65.** **(b)** Lithuanian-born (1886) Jolson's original name was Asa Yoelson.

**66.** **(c)** Andy Cohen replaced Rogers Hornsby in 1928 as the Giants' second baseman, but did not become an outstanding attraction.

**67.** **(c)** The ice hockey award was first donated by Hart's father, Dr. David A. Hart, during the 1923-24 season.

**68.** **(c)** Luckman was All-Pro from 1941 to 1944, and again in 1947. He was elected to the Pro Football Hall of Fame in 1965.

**69.** **(c)** Isaac and Raphael Soyer gained reputations as artists of the Realist school, particularly for their portrayal of life on the Lower East Side of New York. Abraham pronounced his name Shor.

**70.** **(b)** Holman is often referred to as "Mr. Basketball." In 1981 he was inducted into the Jewish Sports Hall of Fame.

**71.** **(c)** In 1926 he donated a concert hall to the Tel Aviv community.

**72. (c)** In the Minor Leagues, Epstein played for Rochester.

**73. (a)** Steinhardt was born in Posen, Poland, in 1887, and settled in Palestine in 1933.

**74. (c)** Szyk died in 1951.

**75. (c)** His National League career batting average was .304.

**76. (a)** In 1952 she was a victim of Senator Joseph McCarthy's witch hunt of suspected Communists.

**77. (c)** English pugilist Mendoza was born in 1764 and died in 1836. He was England's sixteenth heavyweight champion.

**78. (c)** Ross is a member of the Boxing Hall of Fame. He fought and won his battle against drug addiction, a habit he acquired as a result of the use of painkillers to ease the discomfort of wounds suffered during World War II.

**79. (b)** Kling played for many teams but won distinction during his tenure with the Chicago Cubs. He was born in Kansas City, Missouri, in 1875, and died in 1947.

**80. (a)** Stern became the commissioner of the National Basketball Association on February 1, 1984, succeeding Larry O'Brien.

**81. (c)** Accounts of her birth date and original name vary because she was the illegitimate child of a Jewish courtesan and a non-Jew named Bernard or Bernardt.

**82. (b)** Walter Damrosch served as conductor of the New York Metropolitan Opera orchestra.

**83. (a)** Winters won an Academy Award for Best Supporting Actress in *The Diary of Anne Frank.*

**84. (a)** His stage name was derived from his middle name, Edwin. Ed Wynn's television show, *The Ed Wynn Show,* was popular from 1949 to 1959. His son is actor Keenan Wynn.

**85. (c)** Peerce and Tucker were cantors earlier in their careers.

**86. (b)** Chagall, whose original name was Segal, decorated the ceiling of the Paris Opera House and created frescoes for the Metropolitan Opera in New York City.

**87. (d)** Her mother's maiden name was Weinstein-Bacal.

**88. (a)** The players were easily recognized by the Star of David on their uniforms.

**89. (d)**    Arad captured the Silver Medal in judo.

**90. (d)**    Leonard is a member of the Jewish Sports Hall of Fame.

**91. (d)**    Holzman changed her name to Kitty Carlisle, and Peiser changed her name to Lily Palmer.

**92. (b)**    Amy Irving and Ron Rifkin starred in this play by the author of such outstanding works as *Death of a Salesman* and *All My Sons*.

**93. (d)**    The Israeli Philharmonic was founded in 1936 by the violinist Bronislaw Hubermann and inaugurated by Arturo Toscanini. Zubin Mehta, of Indian extraction, became its leader in 1977.

## About the Author

Alfred J. Kolatch, a graduate of the Teacher's Institute of Yeshiva University and its College of Liberal Arts, was ordained by the Jewish Theological Seminary of America, which subsequently awarded him the Doctor of Divinity degree, *honoris causa*. From 1941 to 1948 he served as rabbi of congregations in Columbia, South Carolina, and Kew Gardens, New York, and as a chaplain in the United States Army. In 1948 he founded Jonathan David Publishers, of which he has since been president and editor-in-chief.

Rabbi Kolatch has authored more than a dozen books, the most popular of which are *The Jewish Home Advisor*, *This is the Torah*, *The Jewish Child's First Book of Why*, *The Jewish Mourner's Book of Why*, and the best-selling *Jewish Book of Why* and its sequel, *The Second Jewish Book of Why*. Several of the author's works deal with nomenclature, about which he is an acknowledged authority. *The New Name Dictionary* and *The Complete Dictionary of English and Hebrew First Names* are his most recent books on the subject. Other books by the author include *Our Religion: The Torah*, *Classic Bible Stories for Jewish Children*, *Who's Who in the Talmud*, and *The Family Seder*.

In addition to his scholarly work, Rabbi Kolatch in interested in the work of the military chaplaincy and has served as president of the Association of Jewish Chaplains of the Armed Forces and as vice-president of the interdenominational Military Chaplains Association of the United States.